D0295971

1st edn '83   £4.00

The
MAGIC
GARDEN

*To George Seddon, who taught me how to garden,
along with everything else*

ACKNOWLEDGEMENTS

*I would like to thank the many people who have helped
to get this book to the point where you are reading it:
George Seddon, who encouraged me to write it and then
edited the first draft: Ashley Stephenson, the Gardener
Royal, who was kind enough to spare time from his duties
in order to check the manuscript, which he did with his
usual charm, tact and firmness: Fisons horticultural
consultant David Mann, who was also good enough to
check technical detail: Tom Wellsted, editor of the
bestselling 'Dictionary of Garden Plants', who helped me
with research as did Ann Bonar and Leslie Godfrey who
designed the garden pool.*

*Finally, I must thank my enthusiastic Pilot editor, Piers
Dudgeon, (enthusiastic because he is also a beginner-
gardener) and Mike Ricketts who persuaded me to publish
this book and then designed it for me.*

Text copyright © Florentine Limited, 1983

First published in Great Britain in 1983 by
Macdonald & Co (Publishers) Ltd
London & Sydney

Maxwell House
74 Worship Street London EC2A 2EN

ISBN 0 356 09159 7

Produced by Pilot Productions Limited, London

Typeset by Text Processing, Ireland

Colour origination by Lithospeed (Sales) Ltd, London

Printed in Spain by Printer industria gráfica s.a.

Sant Vicenç dels Horts Barcelona D.L.B. 43257-1982

Line illustrations by Vana Haggerty and Jim Robins

The MAGIC GARDEN

Shirley Conran

MACDONALD & CO
LONDON & SYDNEY

CONTENTS

THE GREAT OUTDOORS

BEGINNERS START HERE

Apart from having a baby, gardening is the nearest thing on this earth to magic. It makes you feel powerful, creative, satisfied, peaceful and fulfilled. It's legal, non-fattening and you can often eat it.

This book is for busy first-time gardeners who have only just discovered the delight of sticking something in the ground and watching it grow like magic; it is for people who haven't much time and want to spend what time they've got lazing in the garden rather than digging it.

6

But the beginner-gardener's first difficulty is knowing where to start - and stop - reading. Most books for beginners seem to have been written by gardeners who forget how all-embracing basic ignorance can be, and that some people actually have to be told that pruning has nothing to do with soaking the rosebushes overnight. If you happen to be a hardy perennial who was raised in a city flat or, until now, has tended to scorn gardening as an occupation for dusty, middle-aged parents, too ancient for anything more exciting, then your first uncertain dip into a gardening book can easily convince you that it's hopeless because you haven't got the Latin, let alone the correct-coloured thumbs. As with ice hockey or the city newspaper pages, if you don't know the basic rules and the language, the whole business can seem too daunting to start.

But it's worth persevering, because once you've started a garden, it's amazingly creative, a constant astonishment and a delight which costs you next to nothing. However small your patch of earth, working in a garden gives you a direct contact with Nature. It's a positive and enjoyable way of releasing the stress of tension and frustration (especially if, instead of sticking pins into wax images, you imagine that each weed is one of your frustrations before you tear it out).

If you're a busy beginner, what you need is a pretty instant garden with minimum work and maximum effect, which will give you the urge to find out and do more about it. So, unless or until your hydrangeas develop a rash of black spots and you have to delve into one of those huge, horticultural "Doctor Spocks" to discover *exactly* what to do about it, here is the basic garden guide .... for indoor gardens as well as the great outdoors.

7

HOW I GREW INTO A GARDENER

This book started several years ago, shortly after I acquired a small, black, damp patch of earth that was attached to my new basement flat. In my mind's eye I instantly saw it as a ravishing mass of pink blossom, rather like an Edwardian lady's hat, so I rushed out and bought some gardening books but unfortunately I couldn't find a single gardening book simple enough to be understood by a really ignorant, impatient city dweller, such as myself.

However, I was lucky enough to have worked on "The Observer" for George Seddon, who writes best-selling garden books. One night I telephoned him in a rage to say that I was living in a basement that faced the wrong way and was shaded by other peoples' trees for 23 hours a day. So, it was as barren as those women in the Bible, and I couldn't find a simple enough book about gardening. They were all full of words like "mulch" and "loam", and I was having to teach myself to garden out of the Oxford Dictionary and the instructions on the back of fertilizer packs, both of which I *could* understand.

George laughed and started to instruct me over the telephone. I did what he said and then, as is my way, I started to experiment by myself. I would telephone George at night, to report, and after a bit he said that I made the most frightful fuss about simple things and I did difficult things with enormous success, because nobody told me that they were difficult. He then suggested that I should write my own gardening book and said I was to start making notes immediately.

"How can I start making notes for a book when I don't know the first thing about gardening?"

"Ah, but you'll *know* how to garden by next year," said George firmly, "and then you won't be able to write the notes, because you will have forgotten what you didn't know. Anyway, you always teach yourself how to do something by writing a book about it. It concentrates your mind wonderfully."

So George taught me to garden by telephone and then I would write my homework notes. I generally gardened at night, in the dark, because that was my only spare time. I did most of it in my kitchen, which quickly started to look like a Habitat-style potting shed. What I liked most was taking cuttings on the kitchen table while watching the ten o'clock TV news; any outdoor stuff had to wait until Sunday.

Before those telephone calls to George, I was unsuccessful with every form of growing things except children. I was a failure even with house plants; I thought that what you should do was give them a lot of water - possibly once a fortnight and notice when they had all dried out, then do it again. There was little horticultural encouragement from the neighbours, whose gardens tended to be worse than mine. They were a literary lot, ranging from Dee Wells and Freddie Ayer to Victor Pritchett and Jonathan Miller. Most of the gardens were admirably adapted to the use to which they were put, which was to accommodate small groups of people with a drink in one hand on Sunday mornings or any summer evening for earnest discussions occasionally punctuated by high-pitched laughter (Claire Tomalin or Jill Tweedie). Apart from this and the neglected children's climbing frames, what everybody wanted was painless gardens in which they could lie horizontal without interruption.

As a matter of fact it doesn't take a lot of time to do the garden, provided you plan a trouble-free one. Before I found myself in the basement flat, I had lived in a place where my bedroom hung five stories above the garden. As I'm shortsighted I felt there was no point in planting stuff I couldn't see, so I just sowed shade grass every year in April and bought blue indoor hydrangeas; when they died I stuck the shrubs around the garden wall, where magically they came up pink the following year. I used to sprinkle-hose them from a great height, feeling like God. It needed hardly any attention apart from a bit of weeding, mowing and watering and I worked out that this simple garden took forty-five minutes a month to look after. (See page 23).

Once I started *proper* gardening and had got used to the fact that I'd better put a bit of careful effort into it, I quickly started to see it as a pleasure, not a chore and I loved everything about it. Like Mary Stewart, the novelist, I found gardening very therapeutic. Her Edinburgh garden is immaculate because whenever she gets stuck in her writing, she goes out and does a bit of vicious weeding. Once, when some disaster hit me and bankruptcy threatened overnight, I telephoned the bank manager to talk about it and ended up wailing, "So what shall I do *now*?" He said, "Why don't you go out and buy some trees?" So I said, "How can I buy trees when I haven't any money?" And he said, "Barclays will lend you money to buy trees because it will cheer you up." And it did. When he retired I gave him a camellia, so that he could think of me every year...as he was weeding it.

Eventually, my problem was rationing the time I spent in the garden, but now it was so seductive that I couldn't bear going away and when I returned I would rush into the garden before unpacking, to see what was happening. Sometimes I would return with gifts for the garden: a marjoram plant from Theodora Fitzgibbon after a cooking trip to Ireland, or wonderful drippy ferns from the Weymouths at Longleat. One of the pleasures of gardening is that giving gifts to people costs very little, and you have the added pleasure of remembering who gave you the cutting every time you look at the plant.

BASIC GARDEN JARGON

If you're just joining the green-thumb set and are intimidated by such words as 'mulch' and 'bolting', here's the Simple Girl's Guide to some mysterious horticultural terms:

Alpines: not plants that need to be grown up a mountain (though they may well have come from there) but specially small, delicate plants, collected from high altitude, and ideal for rockeries or cold greenhouses.

Annual: a plant that is fast-growing and completes its life cycle - from seed to flower to seed - in one year or less.

Biennial: a plant with a life cycle of two years, that is grown from seed. Flowers are not usually produced until the second year.

Blanching: quite simply, excluding light from such plants as celery and endive, to whiten them and improve their flavour.

Bolting: the ruin of many a lettuce - it's when a plant suddenly goes to seed, usually in dry, hot weather.

Brassica: smart name for the cabbage family in general, and related turnips and swedes.

Catch crop: a way to sneak extra foodstuff from the vegetable garden. Sow fast-growing things like lettuce or radish in ground which would other-wise be empty between crops - one empty lot harvested, the other not ready to be planted out. *Inter crop* is a fast-growing crop sown between rows of slower maturing plants.

Compost: either a rich, organic manure that you can make yourself from garden and kitchen waste (see page 28), or a mixture of peat (or soil) and sand, with fertilizers, in which to grow seeds and plants.

Conifer: a tree or shrub which produces its seed in cones (although the yew, which bears berry-like fruits, is included in this group). Almost all of them are evergreen.

Crop rotation: switching around the vegetables you grow from one year to another in a particular place to make sure the soil doesn't get a build-up of disease.

Crown: the top and centre part of certain roots from which shoots appear - in rhubarb, for instance, or lupins or peonies.

Dead-heading: taking dead flowers off plants such as rhododendrons, and roses, which encourages more flowers.

Deciduous: any plants that shed their leaves at the end of the warm season - as opposed to staying evergreen. Evergreen plants shed and replace their leaves, almost imperceptibly, all of the time.

Disbudding: taking off superfluous buds to direct all the energies of the plant into a few superb flowers - a good dodge for producing prize-winning exhibits at flower shows.

Drill: a straight and narrow dent in the ground (usually made with a stick or hoe) in which you sow seed.

Dwarf stock: unrelated to Snow White and her seven constant companions, but no less wonderful. Through horticultural wizardry you can get many of the world's great varieties of apple, pear, peach and plum grafted on a Malling root stock so that trees stay small. Even if you have unlimited space for an orchard, dwarf or semi-dwarf stock takes all the pain out of pruning,

spraying and picking the fruit.

Earthing-up: making a mini-pyramid round a plant usually to blanch it, as in the case of celery, leeks and potatoes, to avoid them from being turned green by the light, or in the case of potatoes to encourage the formation of tubers higher up the stems. If not earthed up, all except for 1 or 2 very close to the surface will remain white.

Evergreen: a tree or shrub that never sheds all its foliage, notably firs, yews, certain oaks, holly, camellia, acacia, certain magnolia, juniper, palm, cedar. Solaces in winter, joys in summer.

Eye: an embryo bud, as in a potato or dahlia tuber; you allow the eyes of potatoes to sprout before putting them into the ground.

Fertilizer: broadly divided into organic matter (meaning non-chemical, natural substances) and inorganic fertilizer (chemical compounds). Organic matter - manure, compost etc.- improves the quality of the soil, as well as adding vital minerals. Chemical fertilizers can be valuable for correcting a specific soil condition, e.g. a nitrogen deficiency. If in doubt test your soil.

Frost: You can expect frosts in Britain between the early autumn and late spring. These are the outside limits for the coldest bits of the country. If you live in warm Devon (or the West of Ireland) the frost season may be from late autumn to early spring.

Fungicide: essential chemical weapon against plant diseases such as blight, brown spot or leaf spot.

Hardening off: gradually getting a plant used to a colder climate. Never take tender plants straight from indoors or from a greenhouse out into the garden: first put them somewhere cool; a well lit garage will do.

Hardy: any plant or person that can live through a British winter. Half-hardy, one which cannot.

Heeling in: putting a plant in the ground temporarily until you are ready to install it properly. The roots are usually put into a shallow trench and covered with earth.

Herbaceous: any plant, from a tomato to a zinnia, that produces soft stems rather than woody ones like shrubs. Some herbaceous plants are annuals, some biennials and some perennials.

Hoe: a tool used to keep the soil free of weeds. Cut them off in their prime with the sharp edge pushed forwards and backwards just below the soil.

Humus: supplied by any organic matter, from animal manure to tree bark or tea leaves, which decomposes in the soil and becomes a dark, rich, sticky substance, that makes soil particles stick together in little groups, leaving gaps for air and water to circulate.

Hybrids: plants that have been specially bred by cross-fertilization, usually for flower colour or size or for bigger, hardier or tastier vegetables. Never save the seed from any hybrid because the plant will not run true to form.

Hydroponics: growing plants without soil - in water and liquid fertilizer.

Insecticide: kills insects.

Mulch: to cover the ground, usually between rows of plants, with any sort of organic, biodegradable material - it could be anything from shredded newspaper between tomato plants to tea-leaves around a house plant. The best materials are hay, straw, peat, grass clippings, sawdust, peat moss or compost. Organic mulching keeps the moisture in the soil, adds nutrition as it decomposes and helps aerate the earth as worms pull it underground. Mulch also keeps down weeds by cutting off sunlight; so do black polythene sheets between plants.

Naturalize: to plant - usually bulbs - in a way that makes them look as though they have grown wild. They are then left for years, to spread.

Node: a joint on a stem from which leaves or bulbs may grow - the nodes on a stick of bamboo show up better than on any other plant, giving it its distinctive appearance.

Perennial: any plant that can go on, more or less, forever. (At any rate, longer than 3 years).

Pinch out: to snip off the tender tip of an unwanted shoot with the fingers to produce more fruit or more flowers.

Plant: Something smaller than a shrub or a tree.

Planting out: moving a young plant from pot or box to open ground.

Pricking out: moving a tender young seedling from the seed box in which it has sprouted to another box or pot where it will have more room to grow.

Propagation: increasing your stock of plants by a number of different ways, in addition to planting seed. (See page 6 3).

Pruning: cutting back a shrub or tree, either to give it a good shape or a crazy shape (as in yew hedges) or to encourage it to produce more fruit or blossom.

Shrub: basically a small bush, it's a plant that has several hard, woody stems (unlike herbaceous plants) and branches but no central trunk like that of a tree.

Time zone: As climate varies not only between the north and south of the country, but also between districts, never think in terms of months for gardening. Rather, think seasonally and in terms of the way your personal plot receives and influences the sun, the wind, the frosts, etc.

Topsoil: the soil on the surface of the garden which is rich in humus, or should be. Underneath is subsoil, which is lacking in bacteria, and infertile. Never mix the two.

Transplanting: removing a plant from one place and planting it again in another.

Variegated: any plant that has two or more colours in leaf, flower or stem. If you want to keep this effect, it's usually important to grow the plant somewhere sunny.

Verbal tip for beginners ... You sow a seed and you plant a plant. You don't sow a plant or plant a seed.

Weed: any plant that is growing where you don't want it. In some Mediterranean countries a geranium is a weed, in many parts of the United States honeysuckle is a weed and so are lots of herbs that we treasure.

Why plants have latin names and what they mean

As there are over 250,000 different plants they have to be referred to by a distinguishing name that all nations can understand. Latin became the *lingua franca* of early botanists all over the world, and some of the names used to consist of as many as six words until the mid-eighteenth century when Swedish naturalist Carl Linnaeus simplified the system.

The first of two words that are generally used to identify a plant, describes the genus or branch of the plant family to which it belongs. It is written with its first letter as a capital letter when followed by the second word. This second word describes the species, i.e. the specific name of the plant, and carries no capital letter.

For example, *Calluna* is the heath genus which belongs to the Ericaceae family, and *Calluna vulgaris* is the specific name for heathers commonly seen growing on the English moorlands.

Sometimes there is a third name, which describes the variety of the plant - a still more specific reference for you to use when seeking a particular plant from nursery or garden centre.

For example, *Calluna vulgaris* 'Beoley Gold' is a particular variety of heather which has golden foliage and white flowers.

Now to get down to the actual business of gardening.

PLAN AN EASY GARDEN
(Horizontal gardening, this)

If you have inherited an unknown garden (bought the house in November) and it doesn't look a tangled, dank mess, try to wait a full growing season, in order to see what surprises may be in store before uprooting everything. But you will probably want to see quick results, and the less you know about gardening the more impatient you are to translate your dreams into reality.

Before you get carried away by romantic notions of gardening there are a few decisions to be taken.

Plan ahead. What I mean by planning ahead may seem pessimistic but is totally realistic. If your backyard will be full of children, dogs and cats (not necessarily yours, either) plan for it. If your garden is going to be a temporary pram stand, play-pen, then outdoor adventure playground, better accept the fact that it may be a good idea to actually plan it as a hell-hole of beaten earth (the children will beat the earth) decaying play frames, old bits of lead pipe, upended flowerpots for racing and discarded bits of old bicycles. Alternatively, level the earth yourself (See page 70) spread a layer of ashes on top and lay old bricks - in patterns if you wish - filling in cracks and crevices by brushing loose earth into them. Old bricks look better than new and can be collected over a period from building sites, skips, etc. Later, plan for the slipped discs of your middle age, and the added leisure of old age when you no longer need to tether children in it but can push your spouse out to grass, to potter about and keep out of your way.

Decide what you can't do. These decisions may be based on the fact that you have no sun, no earth, no time and a surfeit of young animals (some human) that will only wreck whatever you plan, like horticultural black death or phylloxera among the grape vines.

When I first had a garden, everything died because I just kept trying to grow what *I* liked, oblivious of the garden's soil and light. I didn't realize that you really have to choose the plants to fit the garden: the climate, the soil, the way the garden faces, the trees already in it and in neighbouring gardens, and the subsequent sunshine and shade available.

Decide on the amount of *time and money* you are prepared to spend and don't overestimate either.

At this point you decide whether you're going to dig or not to dig, and (if you're like me) you plan a minimum-dig garden, which rules out certain things like vegetables.

Plan to make what you have to do as easy as possible. If you live in the city and don't want the sort of neat little garden that looks like a flowered rug or the chic little garden that looks like close carpeted cement you have to aim for a natural look. The easiest way to do this is to let Dame Nature take over as your gardener. She's free, doesn't complain, you don't get her neuroses dumped in your lap and she doesn't pinch your gin. She knows the job better than anyone else. If you're busy or lazy and can't beat her, you might as well join her. Weeds are only flowers in the wrong places. But the wrong place in which they root is your mind, not your back garden.

Anything green and luxuriant is better than a patch of bare earth. And who wants to spend the next 300 years cultivating the perfect English lawn? I prefer to see nodding buttercups and daisies amidst any green I can grow; the graceful dandelion, with its all too short season - here to-day and fluff tomorrow - dock leaves, waving their verdant heads in the breeze, that sort of thing.

Plant a delicate, white-painted vaguely Victorian metal sofa in the middle of the biggest clump of daisies, adjust a straw hat on your head at a becoming angle, pour lemonade and imagine that Lord Snowdon is about to snap you.

The only problem with weeds is that you can't say to them "*Stop!* That's perfect!" They do tend to take over: but then I'm against any garden that looks too neat.

If you are more ambitious (but not much) plan an orchard-like nature garden with fruit trees and long grass.

If you are one stage *more* ambitious, you might plan a carefree informal (deliberately untidy) garden.

Plant casual clumps of flowering and evergreen shrubs. Grow tall shrubs or plants against any walls, fence or chicken wire and put low spreading carpeting plants in front of them. Encourage long, cool grass then just don't cut it. Grow carpeting plants that cover the ground with lots of thick foliage which keep down weeds. All you have to do is cut the grass twice a year, prune the shrubs, then lift and split up the perennials every 3 or 4 years, when they start getting out of hand. This looks better as a section of a big garden, rather than in a postage-stamp back yard, where it won't look romantic, but neglected.

Of course, you may actually have the time and the urge to do rather more than this: fortunately for you, gardening has become much easier in the past few years. Adam never had a FLYMO, chemical fertilizers, prepared composts, hormone rooting compounds and polythene bags. Today, you don't need any special talent or even much patience to grow a beautiful garden. You only need a little knowledge, a little work, a little patience, a lot of attention to detail, and trouble-free plants.

You can do quite a lot of your gardening by narrowing down your choices: this is done simply by lying with your feet up on a sofa, which is my favourite position for doing anything.

This is also undoubtedly the best position for planning a garden, which purists do on chequered paper, having measured it first. At this point you decide whether you want a little paved patio or a little pond (in which case, you'll have to have a little hill or little bank or decide how else to dispose of the surplus soil). If you work to sculpt the land on a big scale in a big garden that has road access, you can hire a bulldozer and operator by the hour. I promise you, there is nothing so god-like as digging a lake and flinging up a mountain with what you took out before the stew has finished cooking.

The grand plan

When planning a garden from scratch, use graph paper and a soft lead pencil (easily erased).

Check whether there's anything you want to hide, such as the ugly building at the end of it.

Check any existing trees. Do you want to keep them all? Or repair them? Or just reduce the size? (In Britain, within conservation areas, no trees can be removed without official local government permission.)

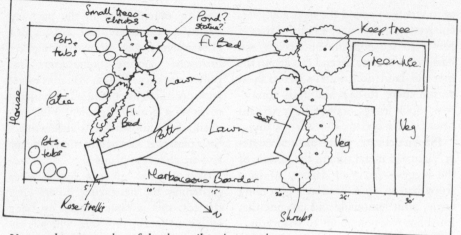

Use graph paper and a soft lead pencil to draw a plan

Decide on any landscaping (shifting the contours - having a grassy bank for wild thyme *here* and a lily pond *there*).

Decide on any excavation work such as patios, walls or irrigation trenches. Decide how to dispose of surplus material. You can't just dump it on the road, it's illegal: telephone the garbage removal department (dustmen) of your town hall, and they will quote for removing it.

If you're using a contractor, don't pay him until the work is completed and ask to *see* his insurance policy, covering you and anyone else, such as neighbours or the council drainage system, for any damage he causes. Get a builder's quotation for the cost.

When your landscaping is complete, plan to check it for drainage problems: rain collects in hollows; water kills a lawn.

This can be corrected by digging a French drain at the bottom of a slope: it's a ditch, 3 feet deep x 1 foot wide. Fill with coarse gravel and add topsoil.

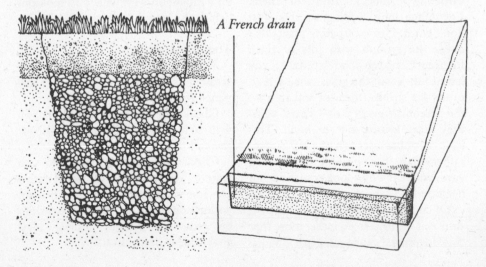

A French drain

16

Now check the weather. Is your patio sheltered from the wind? Which parts of your garden never get the sun and which parts get most of it?

How much sun does your garden get, when and where?

Plan to clear the garden. For instance, take up plants (only in autumn, in Britain), burn off vegetable matter and keep the ash to dig in the flowerbeds. Clear away as little soil as possible.

Check your soil. If it's clay or chalk, plan to get new topsoil, if necessary. Find out how much it costs.

Prepare the ground for planting. This means breaking it up (by spade-work or combustion engine). Spread topsoil over areas for grass or planting, feed the soil.

Then you go shopping.

It is possible to stock a garden by scrounging from friends, but it isn't sensible, for you are likely to end up with a nondescript collection in dubious health. You can be far more discriminating if you buy.

Going shopping

Nature and thousands of nurserymen are on the side of the beginner gardener. Together they provide a lot of flowering plants which look good for very little care and are not easy to kill (touch wood). Plant prices vary enormously. If you're a beginner, don't try to be smart and shop around, pick an old established, reputable nursery. Don't be fooled into buying cheaper plants advertised in newspapers or magazines (at perhaps half the price of a garden centre or nursery catalogue) because you aren't skilled enough to nurse immature plants, you don't want to wait three years to see if some sub-standard plant with an inadequate root system is going to survive, and you can't afford the setback in your self-confidence that a bed of dying plants can generate. Another bit of botanical Latin is *Caveat emptor*: you get what you pay for.

Nothing beats a personal visit, for the beginner. If you are lucky enough to live near a good garden centre, go and choose the plants yourself and see them at their best in the soil of their choice. Don't expect some kindly old gardener to spend hours helping you decide what you want. The staff haven't got the time or the training to educate you, or help you make up your mind. Garden centres are not full of amiable, knowledgeable Percy Throwers, with beards and friendly expressions who will kindly lean on their spades and advise you: they are interested in a) selling b) as quickly as possible c) getting onto the next customer or back into the warm shed. Which reminds me, don't hesitate to write to the manufacturer of any chemical product you need, should the garden centre say they can't get it for you.

How to pick a good garden plant

The plants should be clearly labelled.

Pick out sturdy plants with a full rounded, healthy look: like a dog's nose, a healthy plant doesn't look dry.

Spurn any plants that are yellow, wilting, spindly, straggling, have damaged leaves, look gnawed around the edges, have greenfly or anything else on them.

Shake it *out* of that nasty little plastic container that is so cunningly concealing the root, and have a good look at it. Choose a plant with several small roots, rather than one with one or two larger roots.

Check containerized plants before handing over your money. You do not want a plant with a spiraled root system, because it won't grow well.

If you're *buying shrubs*, try to get a decent shape, i.e. not thin or straggly. Yes, as the man will tell you, you *can* probably prune it to a good shape, but that's going to take a long time - and it will be easier for you to learn how to prune if you know what the thing ought to look like before you begin.

If you're *buying trees*, don't buy tall trees because the roots will be left behind when it's moved, so buy small, young trees. As formerly with debutantes in taxis, not an inch above the kneecap is the rule, if you want it to start growing the year after planting and reach a great height. Try to pick a tree in its second year from seed.

If *buying bulbs*, examine them for pests, fungus and rot.

If you're *buying seeds*, buy fresh, not stale. If there isn't a date on the packet, buy only from a reliable source and don't undo the packet until you want to sow them.

If you have to order by post always buy from a reputable, well-established source. (See list of growers, page 112).

Never buy anonymous plants without a grower's label from greengrocers or supermarkets, because you can't be sure of the quality.

Never impulse buy in a nursery (too fatally easy). Make up your shopping list (still on that sofa) and then, if possible, telephone the nursery to check that they've got what you want: this not only avoids impulse buying but also that situation where the man says he hasn't got *exactly* what you want, but he's got something that's *nearly* the same, and remarkably fine, in his opinion; in this situation, you don't say 'yes' until you have checked out his alternative in a catalogue or this book.

Construct your shopping list thumbing through
THE SIMPLE GARDENER'S UN-COMPUTERIZED CALCULATOR (see p. 30) in order to:
1. Check that the plants will like your soil.
2. Check whether the plants mind any local problem you may have, such as shade, pollution from motorways or factory fumes.
3. How much space they will *eventually* need.
4. *Then* look at the catalogues or visit the nursery.

SMALL IS BEAUTIFUL

Backyard into Courtyard

If you have to be satisfied with a patio, balcony or backyard, you will want to make what is often a pretty grim area as pleasant as possible, and as hospitable in the summer as your living room. Your own back garden is the only place where you can enjoy a summer picnic without ever forgetting the salt and with instant access to shelter when it rains. Turning a dingy backyard into an alluring courtyard is a relatively small job and can be cheaper than caring for a complete garden.

First you need somewhere to sit. Cane furniture is pretty when new but quickly gets weather-beaten if you leave it outdoors. Aluminium Victorian styles, if you can afford them, look lovely when painted white. If you can't afford them, buy junk-shop chairs and paint them white or dark green. They won't last forever outdoors; treat them as annuals, they're cheap to replace.

If you build an 18 inch high x 18 inch deep brick wall across one side of your backyard and lay slate slabs across it that will give you permanent seating. Oil the slate once a year (mineral oil) to keep it gleaming, having scrubbed it when you spring clean.

A variation of this idea is to build a 2 foot high wall, 18 inches away from a brick wall (with draining holes at its base), paint it white and fill it with pelargoniums and lobelia (an ideal solution, incidentally, for the slipped-disc brigade, this no-stoop flowerbed). Both these ideas quickly pull together a 10 foot x 10 foot backyard.

Another idea for a small backyard is to treat it as a small dining room (even if you don't intend to eat there) with a central white table, 4 chairs and a white fibreglass shrub tub in each corner. If possible, paint the walls white up to a height of about 7 - 8 feet, because even when grimy, white looks more crisp, summery and cheerful than gloomy bricks.

*Permanent seating or a raised bed
can transform a
gloomy backyard*

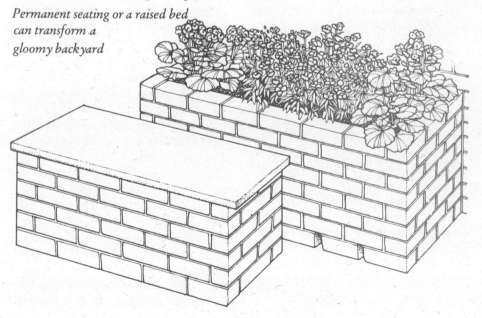

Flower tubs should stand just off the ground; put bricks under them so that water can drain away. Plant them with honeysuckle
lemon-scented verbena
mignonette, for its wonderful aroma
pale mauve heliotrope
petunia

Alternatively, track down an old wooden beer barrel and get holes bored in the side (about 4 inches apart) in 2 rings round the tub. Put the usual layer of broken pottery in the bottom, fill it with LEVINGTON potting compost. In spring, plant strawberry plants in the top and into the side holes. Given plenty of sun you will, with luck, be eating strawberries by late summer.

Hanging wire baskets are fairly easy to organize. Buy a basket, line it with sphagnum moss to hold the soil in place. Fill with LEVINGTON potting compost, plant it with trailing lobelia, orange nasturtium, brilliant pink pelargonium. Hang the basket from a metal bracket, which will keep the basket from leaning drunkenly against the wall; not too high because the soil dries

out very fast and will have to be watered frequently. Good for decorating basement walls.

If you want to light the patio on summer evenings, be prepared for the swarms of moths and mosquitoes that lights will attract; use a cunningly placed architectural spotlight: candles or nightlights protected from the breeze in jars are a good alternative. Put them where no one can knock them over, hanging as high as possible, so that the mosquito convention gathers high above your head. Alternatively, plug indoors, on a long lead, an electric bug disperser, and trail it out to where you're sitting. That's the minimum, weekend transformation scene. Now for more ambitious, glamorous plans which will take a summer to achieve.

A paved courtyard

Consider this for a really small town garden, or bit of backyard, because a small area of grass will fast get trodden to death.

The prettiest courtyard I've ever seen was the size of a small room, and lay beyond the glass doors of a city dining room. The floor was packed with bricks laid in a herring-bone pattern. A mass of winter *Jasminum nudiflorum* grew up and over the 6 foot high walls. An outdoor spotlight shone on the delicate starlike flowers and on the lilies which filled the big tubs.

The most *breathtaking* backyard I've seen was surrounded by factories near Fulham football ground. The owner had simply filled her garden with a tiny turquoise swimming-pool, paved the surrounding area, and had also covered the high brick walls with winter jasmine. Of course, it wasn't cheap but it certainly was spectacular, and added to the value of the house. If you don't want the bother of a swimming pool, you might consider having an informal, shallow pool. (See p. 78).

To pave your courtyard, the cheapest way is to brick it (using old bricks if possible) or cement it (I would get a builder to do this) and then cover as much as possible with tubs. Or you can lay York paving stones (if you can find and afford them. Ask your local nursery, your local town hall or advertise in "The Times" for them). Leave wide gaps between the paving stones, try to lay them *out* of true and fill the gaps between with soil and sand (from a nursery, not builder's sand) in which you can grow small plants. Or you could lay concrete tiles in natural, terra cotta or slate colouring (tell the supplier that you want chipped seconds) or (getting more expensive) pale terra cotta tiles or terrazo (although marble chippings look a bit too *smart* for a garden, I think): they must be laid on a cement bed or on a screeded concrete sub floor.

You might make a French garden. This is fast, attractive and looks professional. First you scorch the earth of weeds with ICI'S WEEDOL. Then you lay a sheet of plastic over the garden (to stifle weeds). Then you lay gravel on it, which a builder's merchant should supply if you can't simply pick it up cheap from the side of the road. Then you poke holes where you want plants (can't have second thoughts once a hole is made, so ponder your plan before starting to knife the plastic). Make sure the sun shines on your holes. Plant your holes with container plants, pick some pleasant, long, reclining chairs and start stirring the Bellinis to celebrate the birth of your new garden.

If the garden has a dingy view, whether it's a factory wall, chicken wire fencing, the back of the garage or anything else that needs screening, grow the Russian Vine, (*Polygonum baldschuanicum*), which not only grows upwards but also rambles over the ground, so can be useful as a weed smotherer. This "art nouveau"-type creeper seems to grow at the rate of a yard a day, although the Botanic Gardens at Kew swear that it's only fifty foot a year. Anyway, it should busily cover unsightly walls in a summer and can be trained over walls, fence or trellis, up the bicycle shed or over the bit of fence that hides your dustbins. It looks a bit forlorn in winter, but it will certainly provide you with a fast cheap curtain of summer green whereas Virginia creeper (very pretty against white walls) or rambler roses, climbing hydrangea, clematis or honeysuckle take longer. Be

cautious with ivy because it gets a stranglehold on flimsy erections, such as trellis, and may pull it over. BUT before planting any of these, check page 61; you might prefer to curb your impatience and grow something slower and more controllable.

Choose a fast-growing angelica

You could surround your backyard with the biggest, fastest growing angelica (grows to 7 feet high) or, if you can find one, a cane-stemmed impatiens, a kind of balsam which grows on thick juicy red stems to 5 feet high, has hand-shaped big leaves, orchid-like mauve flowers and interesting seed pods which break sharply when touched and scatter all over the place, much to the delight of children.

Then all you need do is buy a few trouble-free bedding plants in late spring.

You might prefer to concentrate on a more practical, pretty small garden that you can eat. If so, choose vegetables for their looks rather than their taste or rarity value. Runner beans, with scarlet flowers, make a charming background, rhubarb leaves look steamily tropical, so do artichokes, with pretty blue flowers, and asparagus foliage is irresistibly elegant.

If your backyard is a little bigger, decide whether you need grass, and whether you are prepared to mow it (and where you'll keep the mower). If so, try a slow-growing shade grass or a fragrant little dark green camomile lawn, as at Buckingham Palace, with a magnolia or a fruit tree, centre stage back or to one side.

You might edge your central patch of green with informal (irregular) areas of rosemary, lavender or thyme, interspersed with fragrant mint and taller fennel. Get a couple of low bay trees (not the ones shaped like lollipops) from which you can take cuttings and *voilà*! your own aromatic herb garden. (Herbs are also pretty for lining beds and borders and for softening any hard edges of path or terrace).

For maximum effect in a small space, there are 2 rules for a débutante gardener.

1. The fewer varieties you choose the less you'll have to remember about their care and the more pulled-together the garden will probably look.

2. Pick a deliberate colour scheme, as you would in a room, trying one of the following:

   Whites mixed with yellows - it's fresh and countrylike.

   A mixture of different pinks - they're always glamorous.

   A mass of blues - remembering that you'll have less choice.

   A cheery, old fashioned patriotic mixture of red, white and blue but *not* yellow.

My last garden had a pink scheme, which you may well loathe, but I'm explaining it in detail because it meant I needed to garden seriously only twice a year.

The plan was based on 8 paving stones outside the back door and a patch beyond with a bay tree and an elder bush (for making elderflower champagne in June). The rest was shade grass, pink hydrangeas, pink pelargoniums and *Aucuba japonica*. The evergreen aucuba started off in windowboxes and was teamed with pink pelargoniums in white fibreglass tubs around the patio. When it got bigger the aucuba was removed to the border. My bit of luck. was that both my neighbours had carefully cultivated white rambler roses, which spilled over on both sides and transformed my patch into a bower.

Every spring I sowed 4 oz per square yard of the shade grass. It was hardly the stuff that bowling greens are nurtured on, but it was the right colour green. Every autumn I removed the leaves discarded by neighbouring trees, viciously raked up the grass, scattered seed all over it (see lawns P 68) and watered well. The patch looked messy for a few days then sprung miraculously to life. Every April I bought pots of luxuriant blue hydrangeas for indoors and when they had flowered, I planted them in a growing semi-circle round the garden walls. The following April I clipped off their withered heads: then they grew again; they went in blue and came out pink. It may not have been gardening but it *was* magic. (In fact, the magic ingredient was the soil's acidity.)

EARTH MOTHER

Starting from scratch - whether it is the gardener or the garden - the soil is the first thing that needs attention. Débutante gardeners tend to spend on the wrong things. You need only a few cuttings or seed packets to start a garden. Where your money should go is in the soil, on improving the earth and feeding the plants with manure and fertilizer.

Word of warning

The John Innes Horticultural Institute formulas are excellent - but as anybody is allowed to use them, unscrupulous manufacturers can put any old exhausted, rubbishy earth into smart packs and label it 'JOHN INNES' even if they don't stick to the John Innes formula. Fisons reckon that their peat-based compost is as good as the original John Innes formula: it is the only one sold (as 'LEVINGTON') under the Fison brand and they can guarantee the quality and consistency of it.

Good loamy soil is a mixture of sand and clay and much vegetable matter which is being broken down into humus. To get good soil these ingredients should be present in the correct amounts: they seldom are. Some will be predominantly sandy, clay, chalky, or peaty. Different plants like different soil conditions and what may cause one plant to flourish may cause another to wilt. So, either limit yourself to growing only those plants which actually prefer your conditions, or improve your soil by adding the ingredients it lacks. This is much more expensive and complicated; I would always choose plants to suit the soil, rather than trying to change the soil.

The first step is to analyse your soil to discover what sort of soil it is - the most important question being whether it is alkaline or acid. You can buy a cheap chemical soil-testing kit from your local garden shop. The kit will probably contain a test tube (in which you put your soil sample) some chemical and a colour chart. Mix soil with chemical and when your sample changes colour, you can check from a chart to see how alkaline or acid your soil is. The pH factor is the measure of alkalinity or acidity in your soil. Chalk and lime make the soil alkaline: too much manure, compost or peat will after many years, make the soil acid.

A reading on your testing kit of less than pH7 shows an acid soil; readings higher than pH7 show an alkaline soil.

Most plants will accept a reading of 5 - 6.5, that is slightly acid soil: if the soil is *too* acid you will have problems unless you limit yourself to the plants that tolerate acid extremes. (See P 54 for difficult conditions). For instance, rhododendrons and most heathers will flourish in acid conditions but would perish in a chalky soil - even if you dig in peat.

Food for gardens

Don't expect too much of Nature. She needs your help. Just like other living things, plants are nourished with air, sunshine, water - also food. This is the magic ingredient that in hard-worked private gardens *you* have to supply or your plants will starve, wilt and probably die, just as your children would if you didn't feed them.

The food may be contained in bulky organic material such as animal dung or garden compost, or in chemical fertilizers.

Manure in autumn or early winter with well-rotted farmyard manure, garden compost, hop manure or leaf mould. This organic material will not only feed the soil but will improve its texture and water retaining capacity. Spread 1 wheelbarrow over 12 square yards and fork in.

Be careful to let the manure rot thoroughly. A friend of mine, equipped with humiliating bucket and shovel, trotted after the horses in Hyde Park, then returned home to spread the results on the roses in his tiny garden without allowing the manure to rot. The result was that not only did *the roses* fail to benefit from the mulch, but his family couldn't sit outside all summer, because the garden STANK!

Organic manure decomposes in the soil and becomes humus, which is not that stuff you spread on toast in Nicosia but a dark, rich, sticky substance that improves fertility and soil texture, making soil particles stick to each other in crumbs, leaving gaps for air and water to circulate. Humus really is magic - it helps loose soil retain water and makes soggy soil well-drained.

Mulching

Manure, peat or compost are also spread on the surface of the soil in spring, after the soil has warmed a little, and not dug in. This insulates and keeps the ground moist, smothers weeds, and eventually feeds the soil. To be effective a mulch should be at least 2 inches deep. Peat is often used; it looks and smells pleasant and makes heavy soil easier to work with. But there are many other possibilities, including bark and hops.

Peat

Peat has many uses. If your garden has been neglected apply a 2 inch layer of peat and fork into the topsoil. Apply a ½-inch layer of peat and rake into a seed bed. You can use a peat dressing when seeding a new lawn (1 lb to a square yard). You can also put a mixture of 1 part peat to 1 part topsoil in the hole when planting trees, shrubs and roses. All peat is good peat; but use coarse or fine grade peats for different jobs.

Peat on its own is not a manure. But if you add fish manure to medium low grade sedge peat from your nursery and fork the mixture into the soil you have a real tonic, putting back into the soil, organic matter and essential minerals that the plants use up and the rain washes away.

Where to get organic manure

Animal manure - Fisons *Super Manure* is available from shops and garden centres.

Cowpat, Tyrells Manor Farm, Stoke Hammond, Milton Keynes, Bucks.

Horse, Clavering Composts, Golden Avenue, Angmering-on-Sea, Sussex.

Horse and seaweed, Thomas Elliott, Hast Hill, Hayes, Bromley, Kent.

Fish, The Humber Fish Manure Company, Stoneferry Road, Hull.

Pulverised bark, Bentley Ltd., Barrow-on-Humber, Lincs.

Peat - from any nursery or garden centre.

Compost

You can make your own compost, recycling organic waste to the soil as food. It needn't cost you a penny and it improves your soil.

Basically a compost heap is a pile of carefully sorted, selected rubbish, which decomposes in 3 months or more

How to make a compost heap

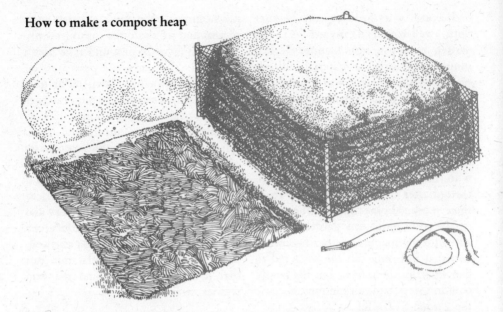

and can then be used to feed the soil. This is how to make one.

1. In an area 7' × 7' dig a 6 inch pit, carefully putting the earth on one side. Fill it with a 6 inch layer of leaves, grass-cuttings, straw and kitchen food waste.

2. Soak with hose (to encourage rotting) then sprinkle with PHOSTROGEN compost maker.

3. Then cover with soil; leave the worms in.

4. Continue to add layers in this order until the compost heap is at least 3 feet high. The last layer should be a 2-inch depth of soil. Keep the heap damp but not wet. It takes at least 3 months to decompose, longer in winter. It shouldn't smell unpleasant or attract flies: properly made, the internal heat burns both out.

Use any organic matter from poultry to birds and rabbits.

You can use weeds; the heat will destroy the seed if you're making the thing properly (though it is advisable to avoid perennial weeds). Use all spoilt plant material, clippings from shrubs and hedges, lawn mowings (provided no weed killer has been used) tree leaves (not more than 10% of the heap).

Use all kitchen waste except grease, bones (which don't disintegrate) and meat (it gets smelly). You can use potato and other vegetable peels and waste matter, orange and other fruit peel, coffee grounds, tea leaves, eggshells, stale bread and cake, leftover vegetables, wood ash (if you have an open fire), torn-up used newspapers (not more than 10% of the heap and don't use colour supplements), tissue and paper wrappings.

Don't put on your compost heap: weeds or grass cuttings for three months after applying weed-killer, coal ash, evergreens or woody material, because they don't disintegrate fast enough.

Either fence your heap on 3 sides with chicken wire attached to 5 poles and add the fourth side when the heap has grown enough to need keeping in its place.

26

Alternatively, cop out with me and buy a compost bin. Bins are not just easier, they are preferable in that a good high temperature is built up and the waste rots down far more effectively. They look a bit like Doctor Who's daleks, or huge 5 foot dark green plastic thimbles. Costs vary· around £12; ROTOCROP do several sizes. By conserving the heat, bins speed the natural organic decomposition in order to convert kitchen and garden waste into rich, dark Christmas pudding coloured humus.

Garden compost has nothing to do with potting compost mixtures which are specially mixed formulas suitable for raising seeds, and for growing plants in pots, window boxes, tubs and hanging baskets. Some are a mixture of soil, sand and peat (e.g. John Innes composts) or consist of blended peat or peat and sand. All include fertilizers.

Why your garden needs fertilizers

Just like you, in order to live, a plant needs light, sun, water, air and *food*. Unlike you, plants can manufacture their own protein. Fertilizers supply the ingredients for the plant to make its' food.

Some fertilizers are organic but most of them are manufactured-experts argue about which is best; some experts say that plants can't tell the difference; so far not one plant has contradicted them.

Inorganic fertilizers are concentrated and act quickly, but overenthusiastic applications may damage your soil, so be careful to follow the manufacturers instructions (one of which is to keep fertilizers out of the reach of children).

Inorganic fertilizers contain concentrated mineral elements, three of which are essential to plants. They are:

Phosphorous which is important to the formation of seedlings, seeds and root growth: you don't want stunted plants.

Potassium which is essential for good colour in flower and fruit, and also good taste.

Nitrogen which is essential to green leaf growth, and also increases size and yield.

The relative concentration of the minerals previously mentioned is clear from the fertilizer label. Some fertilizers are mixed to supply one chemical only, other compound fertilizers have been mixed to a specific formula for specific plants, so read the instructions carefully, and check that your prescription is correct for the plant.

What is not necessarily known is the extent to which your soil is deficient in any or all of these. Nitrogen is quickly washed out of the soil and needs regular replenishment if you want burgeoning, healthy plants. Without your own instant soil laboratory it may be best to use a general-purpose balanced mix of all the important ingredients of a plant's diet: this is called a compound fertilizer and can be bought in handy sizes as GROWMORE.

Don't expect fertilizers to feed the roots when the ground is dry, or during a drought - always water them in.

Don't apply a foliage spray for leaves in strong sunshine, only in the evening or on dull days.

Don't apply a quick acting fertilizer in the autumn, when roots and foliage are dormant because you just waste it.

Don't store fertilizer in a damp place.

Don't apply more than the recommended quantity. An over-rich diet can upset plants, as well as humans.

WHAT TO APPLY	SEASON	METHOD
ORGANIC DRESSINGS		
Decomposed manure (fish: horse: cow: chicken) Peat	In autumn or early winter	Spread, then dig in
Compost (make your own) Peat Leaf mould or spent hops	In spring, when the soil has had time to warm up	Spread 2 inch deep for mulching
INORGANIC DRESSINGS		
PHOSTROGEN - crop booster for vegetables. A compound fertilizer such as GROWMORE	In spring and summer	Sprinkle or spray at roots
Specialist fertilizers for lawns, flowers, roses, vegetables, fruit bushes and trees, (consult your local garden centre).	In late spring, early summer.	Check the package instructions. Spray leaves with fine rose attachment on water can.

DIG, DIG, DIG.

Having done all that you are ready to start digging. Digging is hard work. Not everyone digs. Some people spread a layer of compost over their garden every autumn or spring and sow the seeds in this. Why not, if you can lay your hands on enough good compost.

Avoid digging if you can delegate it, but it must be done to prepare a neglected garden, if you want your garden to grow.

Don't do too much digging on your first day and have a long warm bath afterwards.

Autumn before the frost hardens the ground is good digging time. Never dig when the soil is really wet, sticky and back-breakingly heavy, or when it is baked dry.

Digging is easier if you hold the spade as illustrated

Once into the soil think in terms of turning earth over *rather than straining to lift* it *out of the ground.*

Trenching

The correct way is to dig a trench, spading up the soil and turning it over onto the ground in front. Then you dig trench 2 behind trench 1, but this time you deposit the soil in trench 1. Then you dig trench 3 behind trench 2 and so on, backwards down the garden. I tell you this merely because if you need to do a bit of serious digging, you will eventually find that this is the easiest way to do it.

Don't dig too deep or too enthusiastically but to a one spade depth at a slow, steady pace. Fork manure into the topsoil. The topsoil is the rich part of your earth, like cream-off-the-top-of-the-milk. Never bury your topsoil. Never reveal your subsoil.

If you have a large garden, as opposed to a bath-towel size city backyard, you may prefer to hire a mechanical cultivator (I would). Ask your local garden shop where to locate one. Don't turn over the soil where you plan to put a terrace or paths (you *want* it hard and firm there) and don't use a cultivator on a rainy day or the mess will be terrible.

To clear a lot of really neglected space (including rubble or the remnants of old buildings) you may first need to hire a bulldozer and (usually) an operator, though I know of no more heady feeling than operating one. In one morning you can flatten a mess, scoop out a pond here and deposit the earth to make a rockery there. But it's exceedingly expensive.

Whatever your method, if you are excavating, be careful not to mix your precious topsoil with the useless-for-growth subsoil. Make two separate piles of earth.

THE SIMPLE GARDENER'S UN-COMPUTERISED SHOPPING LIST

One day I expect we'll be into computerized gardening, pressing a button for something white, fragrant and about 3ft 6in tall, that loves acid soil and won't mind shade or city fumes. But, until then, here's a simple checklist for you to choose your plants.

ANNUALS

	Flower time	Soil type	Site

Alyssum
hardy or half-hardy
Suitable edging for rockeries. 3-6in. Fragrant clusters of tiny white, pink, red or purple flowers.

Mid-summer/ early autumn — Well-drained — Sun

Calandrinia
half-hardy
6in. Long, narrow leaves; magenta flowers.

Mid-summer — Light — Sun

Calendula
POT MARIGOLD
hardy
Will often seed itself once planted. 18-24in. Orange flowers in many shades.

Mid-summer — Ordinary soil — Sun

Coreopsis tinctoria (Syn. Calliopsis)
TICKWEED
half-hardy
2-2½ft. Bright yellow with crimson patches.

Mid-summer — Ordinary soil, not too rich — Sun

	Flower time	Soil type	Site
	Mid-summer	Well-drained	Sun

Centaurea cyanus
CORNFLOWER
hardy
Easy to grow. 1-3ft. Blue, mauve, pink flowers.

Clarkia
hardy
Good cut flowers. 1½-2ft. Salmon-pink, purple, white flowers.

Mid-summer	Well-drained, not too rich.	Sun

Convolvulus
hardy
Easy-growing. 15in. Blue or pink flowers.

Mid-summer	Well-drained	Sun

Iberis
CANDYTUFT
hardy
9-12in. Purplish pink or white flowers.

Mid-summer	Ordinary soil	Sun

Delphinium
LARKSPUR
hardy
Dwarf & taller varieties. 1½-3ft. Pink, blue, white flowers.

Mid-summer	Fairly rich	Sun

	Flower time	Soil type	Site

Dimorphotheca
AFRICAN DAISY
hardy or half hardy
Strictly a perennial but
treated as annual. 12-16in.
Daisy-like flowers in apricot,
salmon & other pastels.

Mid-summer — Well-drained — Sun

Eschscholzia californica
CALIFORNIAN POPPY
hardy
Often self-seeding. 9-12in.
Brilliant yellow, orange, red
flowers.

Mid-summer — Ordinary soil — Sun

Gypsophila
BABY'S BREATH
hardy
12-18in. Sprays of small,
white flowers plus other
coloured varieties.

Summer — Preferably chalky — Sun

Helianthus
SUNFLOWER
hardy
To 12ft. Large yellow flowers
with brown central disc.
Requires staking.

Summer/ early autumn — Ordinary soil — Sun

Flower time	Soil type	Site
Mid-summer	Rich	Sun

Lathyrus
SWEET PEA
hardy
As dwarf (9in) or climbing (to 8ft). Versatile, traditional element of cottage garden. Many different colours & very fragrant.

Lychnis coel-rosa var. oculata (Syn. Viscaria oculata)

Mid-summer	Ordinary soil	Sun

hardy
Most species of this genus are perennial. Genus known as campion. 6-12in. Pink, pale blue, carmine or white flowers.

Matthiola
STOCK
hardy or half hardy
Highly fragrant. Try the night-scented varieties. 12-24in. Red/pink, white & yellow.

Mid-summer	Ordinary soil	Sun

Myosotis
FORGET-ME-NOT
hardy biennial
8-12in. Shades of blue, pale pink, white flowers.

Late spring/ early summer	Moist	Sun

Nigella
LOVE-IN-A-MIST
hardy
Good for cutting. 18-24in. Blue, pink or white flowers. Delicate foliage.

Mid-summer	Ordinary soil	Sun

	Flower time	Soil type	Site

Papaver
POPPY
hardy
Will grow to profusion if left
to itself. 2ft but some smaller.
White and yellow flowers as
well as many shades of red.

Early/mid-summer — Well-drained — Sun but shelter from wind

Phlox
half hardy or hardy
Both annuals & perennials
within genus. Great cottage
garden favourite. 6-12in.
Many shades of pink, red or
purple.

Mid-summer — Slightly moist — Sun/partial shade

Reseda odorata
MIGNONETTE
hardy
12-18in. Distinctly scented,
yellowish white flowers.

Mid-summer — Not too loose; plenty of lime — Sun

Tropaeolum
NASTURTIUM
hardy
Good for hanging baskets.
12-18in. Bold orange or red-
dish flowers.

Mid/late summer — Too rich a soil encourages foliage to hide flowers — Sun

GROUND COVERS FOR SHADE

Asarum
WILD GINGER
Evergreen. 4in high; round
aromatic leaves; small, half-
concealed, bell-shaped,
crimson flowers.

Spring — Dry — Light shade

	Flower time	Soil type	Site

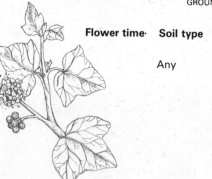

Hedera
IVY
Evergreen. 4in high. Small, glossy leaves in various forms, including variegated varieties.

| | Any | Heavy shade (though variegated forms are much less tolerant of extremes) |

Mahonia repens
CREEPING MAHONIA
Evergreen. 6-9in. Tiny yellow blossoms followed by black berries.

Spring — Dry — Light shade

Pachysandra terminalis
Evergreen. 9-12in.; shiny saw-toothed leaves; small white flowers. A silver marked form, 'Variegata' is also available.

Spring — Dry — Heavy shade

Rubus nepalensis
CREEPING RASPBERRY
Deciduous. 6-9in. Shiny, clover-like leaves; white flowers; red fruits. *Rubus* 'Tridel', more often grown, is illustrated here.

Early summer — Dry — Light shade

Vinca major
PERIWINKLE
Evergreen. 1-2ft. Dwarf form (*Vinca minor*). Small oval leaves; bluish-purple flowers. Also good in hanging baskets.

Late spring — Most soils — Shade

HARDY PERENNIALS

	Flower time	Soil type	Site

Aster novii belgii
MICHAELMASS DAISY
To 3ft with dwarf hybrids to 15in. Many varieties, with white, pink, red, blue and purple flowers. Prone to mildew that can be aggravated by drought.

Late summer/ early autumn — Moist — Sun

Campanula
BELLFLOWERS
Usually from 18-36in. Alpine varieties to 6in. Flowers usually in shades of blue.

At various times in summer. Plant a variety for continuity. — Well-drained — Sun or partial shade.

Delphinium
To around 5ft. Blue, pink, mauve and white flowers; large, deeply furrowed leaves. Good border plants; plant about 18in apart.

Mid-summer — Rich and deep (though some prefer a lighter soil) — Sun

Hemerocallis
DAY LILY
To 2-3ft. Long, elegant leaves; a wide range of flower colours from lemon-yellow to copper-pink in abundant clusters.

Mid/late summer — Most types but preferably moist — Sun

36

	Flower time	Soil type	Site

Pelargonium
GERANIUM
P. peltatum 'King Edward VII'
illustrated here. Cherry-rose,
large flowered, robust variety of the ivy-leaved pelargonium.

	Summer and autumn	Rather stony soil or rich mixture in pots	Sun

Phlox
Usually to 2½-3ft. A wide,
subtle range of flower colours from salmon pink
through orange and lavender
to rich crimson; white
varieties also available.

	Mid/late summer	Light, but not too dry	Sun or par-tial shade

CLIMBERS
See also Jasmine, Lonicera
(honeysuckle)

Clematis
Varieties may be deciduous
or evergreen. To 10-20ft. A
variety of leaf forms; flowers
equally varied, usually in
shades of blue or purple with
some white or yellow
varieties.

	Spring onwards according to type.	Limey, with plenty of leaf mould. Keep moist.	Sun or partial shade (try to keep roots shaded)

Ercilla volubilis
To 10-15ft; leaves tough,
thick and rounded, inconspicuous purplish flowers.
Grows quickly, makes good
ground cover. Evergreen.

	Spring	Well-drained.	Sun or shade

Hydrangea petiolaris
To 50ft; heart-shaped leaves;
large white flowers in clusters. Tolerates urban pollution. Deciduous climber.

	Early summer	Most types. Keep well moistened.	Sun or shade, preferably not a south-facing wall

	Flower time	Soil type	Site
Pileostegia viburnoides To 20ft; leaves large; flowers small, creamy, in clusters. Slow growing. Evergreen.	Late summer/ autumn	Most types	Sun, shade or north facing wall
 **Polygonum baldschuanicum** **RUSSIAN VINE.** Deciduous climbers. To 20-50ft; sprays of small white flowers. Very quick-growing (known as the 'mile-ə-minute' plant).	Mid-summer mid-autumn	Ordinary	Sun
Wisteria A vigorous deciduous climber that needs support if grown against a wall. To 20ft or more. Abundant mauve or white flowers. Some species (*W. sinensis*) are scented.	Late spring/ early summer	Loam, likes moisture	Sun

CARPETING PLANTS AND LOW PERENNIALS   See also Erica

	Flower time	Soil type	Site
 **Anthemis nobilis** **CHAMOMILE** Hardy herbaceous perennial. Dense, 1in cover of closely matted plants. White, daisy-like flowers. Interesting alternative to small conventional lawns, very fragrant when leaves are crushed.	Summer	Well-drained	Sun
Aubrieta Surface spread of 10-12in per plant. Pink, blue or purple flowers. Prune after flowering to improve density and growth. Alpine perennial. 	Late spring/ early summer	Well-drained with plenty of lime	Sun. Good for planting on top of stone walls

38

	Flower time	Soil type	Site

Aquilegia
COLUMBINE
Alpine perennial. To 6-10in,
spread 3-4in per plant. White,
pink, red, blue or purple
flowers. Will need replacing
after 3 years.

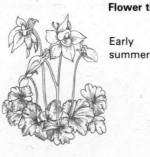

Flower time	Soil type	Site
Early summer	Not too dry	Sun or partial shade

Dianthus alpinus
PINKS. ALPINE
To 6-9in; spread 6-10in per
plant. Pink, crimson or white
flowers. Be sure to specify
the alpine variety as this is a
large genus.

Flower time	Soil type	Site
Mid-summer	Well-drained and limey	Sun

Gyposophila repens
To 6in; spread around 12in
per plant. Various shades of
pink flowers; narrow
glaucous leaves. Good for
trailing over rocks. Plant
during construction of rock
garden. Alpine trailer and
creeper.

Flower time	Soil type	Site
Mid-summer		Sun

Hypericum calycinum
ROSE OF SHARON
Deciduous or semi-ever-
green shrub. To 18in, wide-
spreading; glowing yellow
flowers; oval leaves,
aromatic when bruised.

Flower time	Soil type	Site
Mid-summer	Can tolerate very dry, chalky conditions	Sun or shade

Lobelia
Trailing half-hardy annuals
and perennials. The South
African annual *L. erinus*
grows to 6in. A trailing plant
in many shades of blue
flowers.

Flower time	Soil type	Site
Summer	Moist	Sun

EVERGREEN SHRUBS

	Flower time	Soil type	Site

Aucuba japonica

To 5-8ft; similar spread. Leathery, oval leaves; purple flowers; red berries. Excellent for town and seaside gardens.

Fl. early autumn
B. autumn

Any soil

Shade beneath deciduous trees

Berberis darwinii

To 8-10ft; wide-spreading. Small holly-like leaves; orange yellow flowers; purplish berries.

Fl. late spring
B. late autumn

Any soil except saturated

Full sun or partial shade

Berberis stenophylla

To 10ft: wide-spreading. Narrow, small leaves; golden flowers; blue berries.

Spring

As above

As above

Buxus sempervirens

Box to 15ft. Shiny oval leaves (some varities have yellow markings). Good for hedges and topiary.

Sun or light shade

Callistemon citrinus
BOTTLEBRUSH PLANT

To 15ft. Flowers consist entirely of red stamens.

Early summer

Well-drained fertile

Sun, shelter

Neil Holmes

A basement garden
*Paint walls white – up to a height of about
7-8 ft. Even when grimy, white walls look
more crisp, summery and cheerful than
gloomy bricks.*

Jerry Harpur

First you need somewhere to sit.
*Aluminium Victoria styles look lovely
when painted white. If you can't afford
them, buy junk-shop chairs and paint them.*

*If you want to light the patio use a
cunningly placed architectural spotlight:
candles or nightlights protected from the
breeze in jars are a good alternative.*

Neil Holmes

Jerry Harpur

You might prefer a French garden.
*First scorch the earth of weeds with ICI's
WEEDOL; then lay a sheet of plastic, a
layer of gravel, and poke holes where you
want plants.*

*Pick a deliberate colour scheme as you
would in a room.*

Jerry Harpur

Neil Holmes

Vita Sackville West's famous White Garden at Sissinghurst. My last garden had a pink scheme; see page 23.

	Flower time	Soil type	Site

Camellia japonica
To 20ft. or more; wide-spreading. Many varieties with red, pink, white or variegated flowers, which are susceptible to frost.

	Flower time	Soil type	Site
Camellia japonica	Late winter/early spring	Lime-free	Moderate shade. Not in hot south-facing positions. Because of frost problem, also avoid east-facing position.

Ceanothus burkwoodii
CALIFORNIAN LILAC
To 20ft; wide-spreading. Blue flowers. Prune lightly after flowering. Deciduous species is *C. dentatus*. Among hybrids is the fragrant 'Gloire de Versailles' illustrated here.

Flower time	Soil type	Site
Late summer/autumn	Well drained	Sun but sheltered

Cistus
ROCK ROSE
To 4-6ft; wide spreading; pink or white, purple and magenta flowers with crimson or yellow blotches. Very free-flowering.

Flower time	Soil type	Site
Early/mid summer	Light, well-drained	Full sun

Clianthus
C. formosus is procumbent, *C. puniceus* a climber. Red, pea-pod-like flowers; small clustered leaflets.

Flower time	Soil type	Site
Late spring/early summer	Light, well-drained	Full sun

Cotoneaster
Both small (to 5ft) and large (to 15-20ft) varieties. Small white flowers, scarlet berries.

Flower time	Soil type	Site
Fl. early summer B. late autumn	Any	Sun or shade

	Flower time	Soil type	Site

Daphne

To 3-4ft. Very fragrant; pink flowers (sometimes white). *Daphne mezereum* and *D. laureola* are poisonous, especially bark and berries.

Spring/early summer — Moist, well drained loam. Keep roots cool with plenty of leaf mould — Sun or partial shade.

Elaeagnus

To 8-10ft, Attractive, glossy leaves with gold/rust splashes; fragrant pale yellow flowers. Makes a good hedge.

Autumn — Well drained — Full sun

Erica
HEATHER

Many varieties, from low shrubs to carpeting plants; small flowers, usually pink or white.

Spring or autumn according to variety — Normally acid, although *E. carnea* is lime-tolerant. — Sun

Escallonia

From 6-12ft. Small pink or white flowers.

Mid-summer — Rich, either acid or chalky — Sun

Eucalyptus globulus
GUM TREE

Highly aromatic shrub. Small blue-grey leaves. Needs cutting to 18in every spring to keep bushy.

Both dry and moist — Sun

	Flower time	Soil type	Site

Euonymus europaeus
Spindle tree
Usually to 8-10ft. Narrow oval leaves with brilliant autumn colours, pinkish fruit.

Flower time	Soil type	Site
B. autumn	Very tolerant	Sun or shade.

Fatsia japonica
To 12ft but usually less. Creamy flowers in clusters; large, lobed leaves. Tolerant of urban pollution.

Flower time	Soil type	Site
Autumn	Any	Open, but sheltered from strong/cold wind/draughts.

Garrya elliptica
To 8-12ft; wide-spreading. Dense, greyish catkins in mid-summer on male plants (less pronounced on female)

Flower time	Soil type	Site
	Well drained	Sun or partial shade; sheltered

Gaultheria
Rarely more than 1ft high; creeping habit; small white or pink flowers followed by berries.

Flower time	Soil type	Site
Different species summer & autumn	Preferably acid	Sun or partial shade

Griselinia littoralis
To 20ft. Medium sized oval leaves; small greenish flowers. Useful hedging plant.

Flower time	Soil type	Site
Late spring	Ordinary or chalky	Needs some shelter except in very mild conditions.

	Flower time	Soil type	Site

Halimium
To 3ft; wide-spreading. Small grey leaves; small, bright yellow flowers with wine-coloured blotches at base.

	Flower time	Soil type	Site
	Mid-summer	Well-drained	Sun, shelter

Hebe
9in to 5ft, depending on variety; wide-spreading. Small rounded/waxy leaves; small flowers in spikes, lilac, purple, white, blue, crimson, red.

	Flower time	Soil type	Site
	Mid-summer late autumn	Well-drained	Sun. Some are tender, but all grow well in milder or seaside areas.

Hoheria angustifolia
To 20ft. Long, serrated leaves; small white flowers in clusters.

	Flower time	Soil type	Site
	Mid-summer	Well-drained	Sun or light shade

Hypericum
ST. JOHN'S WORT
To 1½ft. Golden yellow flowers, broad oval leaves. Good ground cover for dry, shady spots.

	Flower time	Soil type	Site
	Mid-summer	Well-drained	Sun or light shade

Ilex
HOLLY
To 20ft; wide-spreading; glossy, thorny leaves (sometimes varigated); bright red berries, inconspicuous flowers. You *must* grow male and female plants together for cross-pollination to occur; makes good hedges.

	Flower time	Soil type	Site
	B mid-winter	Any	Can tolerate exposed conditions

45

	Flower time	Soil type	Site

Jasmine
Vigorous climber to 20ft. Clusters of white flowers from pink buds, very fragrant. Clusters of leaflets. Slightly tender.

Mid/Late summer — Any well-drained — Facing south

Juniper
Some species prostrate, others erect; narrow, needle-like leaves, usually bluish-grey.

Any — Open

Kalmia latifolia
CALICO BUSH
To 25ft, much less in temperate climates. Thick, shiny leaves; large clusters of pink flowers. Good foliage plant for all seasons.

Mid-summer — Well mulched — Dry shade

Laurus nobilis
BAY TREE
To 20ft; wide-spreading. Glossy, aromatic leaves used in cooking. Can be grown in containers.

Any — Sun or partial shade

Ligustrum
PRIVET
To 10-20ft; small oval leaves; fragrant white flowers; some varigated forms. Greedy, thirsty roots.

Mid-summer — Any. Will tolerate poor, dry soils — Adaptable-sun, shade or exposed

	Flower time	Soil type	Site

Lonicera
HONEYSUCKLE
To 7ft; wide-spreading.
Some varieties are climbers;
mostly creamy-white flow-
ers. Prune after flowering.

Mid-summer — Any — Sun (shrubs) partial shade (climbers)

Magnolia grandiflora
To 20ft; wide-spreading:
glossy leaves; large creamy-
white globular flowers noted
for fragrance. Tolerates
urban pollution. Treat fleshy
roots gently.

Mid-summer — Any rich soil — Sun, shelter from wind

Mahonia japonica
To 8-10ft. Large multiple
leaves (some thorny); fragrant yellow flowers.

Winter — Any but chalky — Sun or partial shade, shelter from wind

Olearia
To 6-10ft; wide-spreading.
White daisy-like flowers.
Good for town gardens.

Mid-summer — Well drained, especially sandy or chalky — Sun

Osmanthus
To 10ft; Very bushy; small
oval toothed leaves;
abundant white, jasmine-like
flowers, very fragrant. Slow
growing.

Mid-spring — Any — Sun or a little shade, shel-ter from wind.

47

	Flower time	Soil type	Site

Pernettya

To 5-7ft. Small white flowers
followed by white, pinkish or
mauve berries. Grow male
and female together for
flowers and fruit.

Early summer — Moist, lime-free — Sun or partial shade

Phlomis fruticosa
JERUSALEM SAGE

To 3½ft, spreads wider;
greyish, downy leaves;
spikes of yellow flowers.

Mid-summer — Well-drained or chalky — Sun, needs shelter

Pieris

To 10ft, some taller; fairly
wide-spreading. Rich green
foliage.(*P. formosa forrestii*
has brilliant red new leaves);
white pendulous flowers.
Good companion for rhodos.

Mid-spring — Lime-free — Shade, well sheltered

Prunus lusitanica
PORTUGAL LAUREL

P. laurocerasus (laurel). To
15-20ft, similarly wide-
spreading. Ovally pointed
leaves; white flowers in long
spikes, scented; *P. laurocerasus* has large leathery leaves.
Good hedging plants.

Early spring — Any — Tolerate exposed positions

Quercus ilex
HOLM OAK

Evergreen tree. To 50-70ft.
Oval, glossy but good
hedging plants for exposed
areas.

Moist. well-drained — Sun or shade

DECIDUOUS SHRUBS

	Flower time	Soil type	Site
Buddleia davidii **BUTTERFLY BUSH.** To 9-12ft; equally wide-spreading. Large spear-like leaves; spikes of purple, bluish, crimson or white flowers.	Late summer	Light	Sun
Buddleia globosa To 12ft; wide-spreading. Long, spear-shaped leaves; small, orange ball-like flowers. Lightly prune after flowering.	Late spring/ early summer	Any light soil	Sun
Hydrangea To 3-4ft, some taller; wide-spreading. Large heads of pink, red, blue or white flowers.	Summer/ early autumn	Most kinds	Sun or partial shade
Forsythia To 8ft; spreads up to 12ft. Lavish clusters of yellow flowers.	Early Spring	Ordinary	Sun or partial shade
Viburnum **DECIDUOUS OR EVERGREEN SHRUB.** Usually to 8-10ft, but some smaller varieties. Long, furrowed leaves, fragrant white flowers; blue or red berries.	Fl. spring/ early summer	Rich and moist, including chalk	Sun or partial shade

HEDGES

See also *Ilex* (holly), *Prunus lusitanica* (Portugal laurel)

	Flower time	Soil type	Site

Crataegus
HAWTHORN.
Deciduous small tree. To 15-20ft; similar spread. Clusters of white flowers followed by red berries. Plant 1ft apart for dense hedge.

Early summer — Most kinds — Open sun

Cytisus
BROOM.
Deciduous shrub. To 8-10ft; spread 6-9ft. Yellow; fragrant flowers.

Summer — Well drained — Full sun

Fagus sylvatica
BEECH.
Deciduous tree. To 70ft or more; keep back by regular clipping. Oval, wavy-edged leaves, clusters of green flowers. Trim in mid-summer to retain leaves until spring.

Spring — Sand, chalk or ordinary — Open sun

A TOUCH OF THE WILD

My private definition of a wild garden is what will grow in my garden without me doing anything about it. Wild gardens thus defined are no problem, except for the difficulty of maintaining the correct degree of wildness. Another problem with this sort of garden - full of verdant growth dotted by sculpturesque thistles and dock leaves, with daisies and buttercups nodding their graceful heads - is that the neighbours howl that *your* weed seed goes in *their* garden. But, as I've already said, a weed can be simply a flower that you decide you don't like.

However, neighbourly wrath should remain dormant if you grow a wild orchard garden, which is the easiest garden of any size. Plant it with bulbs which will naturalise themselves in the grass. The grass will not need constant cutting and once you have planted bulbs they will come up every year, and multiply underground. Plant as early as possible in autumn. People often leave it until too late and some bulbs need a long time to establish a good root system.

Remember that you can't cut the grass while the bulb foliage is still growing. The foliage must be allowed to die down, its goodness feeding the bulb before the resting season.

Planting depths vary according to the size of the bulb; they are reckoned from the top of the bulb. In very loose, free-draining soil bulbs should be planted up to an inch deeper.

You can get a special bulb planter for planting in grass to make a neat hole of the right shape. This is *very important*: there should be no air pockets beneath the bulbs. Plant bulbs with the sharp end pointing upwards.

A bulb planter

Don't plant them under dense evergreen trees because they won't get enough light to grow.

When flowering has finished, don't pick the leaves, but let them die naturally. The newly developing bulbs draw nourishment from them.

Narcissus, Lily of the valley, autumn Crocus and winter Aconite.

When you can expect to see them:

In Spring: Daffodils and Narcissus. Plant 3-4 inches deep and 3 inches apart.
Glory of Snow (*Chionodoxa* species). Plant 3-4 inches deep and same distance apart.
Grape Hyacinths (*Muscari* species). Plant 3 inches deep and 3 inches apart.

Early Summer: Alliums. Plant 2 inches deep and 2 inches apart. Lily of the Valley (*Convallaria majalis*). The young planting crowns should only just be covered with soil and planted 12 inches apart. They will flower 18 months after planting.
Bluebells (*Endymion* species). Plant 3 inches deep and 3 inches apart.

Fair Maids (*Ranunculus* species). Plant the tubers, claw downwards, 3 inches deep and 4 inches apart.

In Autumn: Autumn Crocus (*Colchicum* species). Plant 3 inches deep and 2 inches apart.

Late Winter: Winter Aconite (*Eranthis* species). Plant corms 2 inches deep and 2-3 inches apart.
Snowdrops (*Galanthus* species). Plant 3 inches deep and 1 inch apart.
Crocuses. Plant 3-4 inches deep and 2 inches apart.

Hyacinths and the Dutch tulips are not suitable for naturalizing in grass, but tulip species can be naturalized. Plant 4 inches deep and up to 6 inches apart. They will flower in spring. In other parts of the garden hyacinths should be planted 4-5 inches deep and 9 inches apart.

PROBLEM CONDITIONS

A what-to-plant guide

In order to live, plants need light, warmth, water, air and food, and each plant differs in its requirements of these. Plants have evolved so that physically they are adapted to survive in the conditions of their place of birth. It may be an Alpine peak or a hot, humid tropical rainforest.

Even neighbouring gardens differ in the growing conditions that they offer plants (how much sun they get, wind, etc.), but generally it is worthwhile to see what thrives in the plot next door.

Here are lists of plants that might not see the problem conditions of your garden as anything less than an ideal climate.

There are plants for virtually every condition. In general it is better to grow those that are suited to prevailing conditions than to try to alter them. Make life easier for yourself by going with the soil, not against it. Discover its basic nature, add plenty of well-rotted compost (humus has the magical property of helping drain soggy soils and making loose, free-draining soils more water-retentive), and grow plants suited to it.

Plants for shade

Trees. All trees require open sky above them in order to develop their full, natural shape, flower or fruit. Some will accept shade from other trees when still young - oak and beech are typical examples. But in a relatively small garden, shade is generally due to buildings; if they cut out the sun altogether there is little that will grow. Even the holly and the yew that grow wild in partial shade make far better trees (and produce more berries) when given some light.

Here are some shade-bearers that tolerate shade to a degree: Douglas fir, silver fir, Lawson cypress (though the best coloured forms are most sensitive to shade), Western hemlock, yew, holly - the Highclere hybrid 'Golden King' is particularly recommended, though its berries will be sparse in dense shade, as is box (but only as a shrub). Finally, the hornbeam and beech do quite well in side-shade.

Shrubs. Most problematic is *dry* shade, where little colour will survive. Dry shade is created by thirsty, full-leaved trees and hedges that take enormous amounts of moisture from the soil and create severe planting problems beneath them. A layer of well-decomposed compost, peat, bark or leaf mould spread over the soil (gardeners call this a mulch) helps retain moisture in a bed. In dry shade, the ivies, the Chinese non-thorny bramble (*Rubus tricolor*), and the sarcococcas (with their dark, evergreen leaves and early clusters of small, white, sweetly scented flowers) are possible solutions. But the first two have little respect for smaller, weaker plants struggling for survival in the vicinity. You might also try the butcher's broom (*Ruscus aculeatus* in the catalogues). Plant a male plant near to a female plant and cherry-red berries will occasionally brighten its diminutive, scale-like leaves. Where lack of moisture is not a problem, there are many colourful shrubs from which to choose:

Hydrangeas (*Hydrangea serrata* 'Grayswood' for late summer and autumn), *Daphne bholua* 'Gurkha' (for late winter/early spring) are good, as are the rhodos, dogwoods and viburnums that grow in shade in nature. Both rhododendrons and azaleas provide a wide choice of colour, but do prefer an acid soil.

Ferns. After moss they are the first to grow in damp, dark caves. They dislike a waterlogged soil and prefer slightly acid conditions. Ferns may be tall and stately or delicate and diminutive, but whatever size they make marvellous foils for pretty flowers and can be used to cover the bare soil of spring bulb beds, dying down as the bulbs begin to perform.

Herbaceous perennials. Hostas will provide a happy solution for most of the year, leaving the stately cimicifugas, brilliant astilbes, and creamy white aruncus to add variety of size, shape and form. There are also many shade-loving alpines, dwarf azaleas and daphnes from which to choose - an acid soil is preferable, but you could always build a special bed of peat.

In dry shade, the periwinkle is the best bet and very useful for covering large areas of dry, shaded ground. The saw-toothed leaves and white spring blooms of *Pachysandra terminalis* could provide interesting relief, but in very dry areas no display of flowers will last long.

Annuals and bulbs. Snowdrops, winter aconites and cyclamen are the best choice for shaded areas. Annuals are out altogether, though they can of course be container-grown in sunny parts of the garden and moved into shady parts for a few days at a time.

Foxglove and honesty (both biennials) are pretty good in shade and there are many other bulbs that will tolerate light shade provided they receive some light while their leaves are in active growth and they are kept warm and dry during their summer rest period: tulips, daffodils, and crocus all grow naturally in the dappled shade of leafless, deciduous trees in the spring.

Plants for an acid soil

These plants that prosper in soil that is one or two points below a pH7 reading on a soil-testing kit (available at nurseries or garden centres).

Rhododendrons. They vary in size from small to almost tree size: *Rhododendron fictolacteum* with its pale pink or white spotted flowers can grow to 30 ft; *R. griersonianum* with bright scarlet trusses makes a good, medium-sized bush; and there is a wide range of dwarf plants for small gardens.

Queen of the lilies. This flowers when the rhodos begin to fade (in late summer and autumn) and it is not alone amongst lilies for its tolerance of acid conditions.

Azaleas. Related to the rhododendron, these are often more brightly coloured in flower.

Heathers. A marvellous range of colour, and good subjects for a tapestried bed of their own.

Camellias. They flower from late winter to mid-spring when there is little else in bloom.

Witch hazel. Again, its sweetly scented, yellow flowers appear when the garden is at its most dull.

Most woody plants (trees and shrubs) prefer a soil that is slightly less than pH7, but here are some trees that do especially well in more obviously acid conditions:

The maple. But not all of them. The Norway maple (*Acer platanoides*) likes acidity as does the related sycamore (*Acer pseudoplatanus*) - try the form 'Brilliantissimum' for a small garden.

The Lawson cypress. There are many different forms, including a whole range of dwarfs.

The hawthorn. A late spring blossom.

The Chilean firebush. Embothrium coccineum is a striking sight wreathed in brilliant scarlet, tubular flowers.

The Japanese crab apple. Malus floribunda is a reliable, foaming mass of white flowers in the spring.

Spruce, pine, oak, and rowan will also do well in an acid soil garden.

Plants for an alkaline soil

Its important to realize that soils registering close to pH6 - 8 support a wide range of plant life; real difficulties only arise beyond these points. Most annuals and perennials accept some lime, but the perennial peony is noted for its tolerance to lime. Lawns are a problem, and must be fed regularly with acid-type fertilizers or they will only provide scant cover. Here is a selection of plants that tolerate soils with enough lime to register above pH7 on a soil-testing kit:

Trees. The beech, horse chestnut and hornbeam - the last being the most preferable for a small garden. The hawthorns sustain interest with their spring colour and autumn berries. Another tree for a small garden is the maple, *Acer negundo*, not only small for a tree but upright rather than spreading in its growth. Then, of course, the yew prefers an alkaline soil, but remember that it is poisonous to children.

Shrubs. One of the best-known barberries, *Berberis darwinii*, makes a fine display with its small, glossy, evergreen leaves and orangy, yellowy springtime flowers. It has the added advantage of being an ideal foil for stray dogs and cats. Among the buddleia you will find a wide range of forms; they're famous for attracting butterflies. Again, fuchsias are a colourful, graceful 'must' for all limey soils, and if you need a climber try the scented virgin's bower: the *Clematis flammula* prefers its roots in the shade if it is to lift its flowers to the sun.

Plants for dry soils

If dry soil is your particular headache and you want to see how a real professional copes with the problem, visit Beth Chatto's garden near Colchester in Essex. It is open to the public at certain times and there is a highly successful nursery attached. The address is White Barn House, Elmstead Market, Colchester, Essex. If you cannot visit, write and ask for her plant lists.

Free-draining, sandy soils can be improved by spreading a layer of well-rotted compost, pulverized bark, or leaf mould all over the beds. This will help prevent excessive evaporation of moisture from the soil surface.

Commonly known, drought-resistant plants include wallflowers, antirrhinums, lavender, alyssum, thyme, aubrieta. Nature has given them built-in mechanisms to enable them to survive without too much moisture.

Among trees and large shrubs, you could include the juniper, the bay tree, or the Mt. Etna broom (in fact any of the broom family, *Cytisus*). The sun or rock rose (*Cistus*) grows wild in the Mediterranean region, Spain and Portugal and is well adapted to drought conditions; it flowers in succession through most of the summer.

The holly bears up well, as do the Austrian pine, Holm oak, and yew.

Holm oak

Among the smaller plants, as alternatives to those mentioned above, are the herb shrubs sage, santolina and rue. For colour the rugosa rose is exceptional in flower and its lustrous red hips make it a good plant for much of the year. It is also good hedge material.

Plants for wet soils

Few plants will grow in stagnant, waterlogged soil, but see page 83. If your garden is just soggy, not permanently puddled, peat or well-rotted compost will improve its texture and improve drainage. Dig the ground thoroughly in the early autumn and work the drainage material in. Pure gypsum (obtainable from garden suppliers), or coarse grit from builders' merchants also work well.

If you have a soggy garden built on a slope you can improve the drainage by digging a hole 4ft across and 4ft deep at the lowest point. Half fill it with big stones, old bricks, bits of flower pots, anything porous. Then fill to 6in from the top with pebbles, and cover with topsoil.

There are other more complicated drainage methods, often quoted in the encyclopaedias, but if your garden needs these get expert advice and help. Your local nursery can probably recommend a qualified horticulturalist (check this on his writing paper). This sort of advice shouldn't be more expensive than 4 bottles of Scotch. Beginners facing an unscheduled bog *need* expert advice. You cannot afford to go expensively wrong at this early stage.

Trees. The classic tree for wet ground is the willow; it drains moisture out of the soil, and into the atmosphere through its leaves, at an alarming rate. But beware all such 'natural' drainers in times of drought - besides willows, these are poplars, elms, ash and oak. They can extract enough moisture from the soil to cause it to shrink even to the point of upsetting a nearby building. Always remember that tree roots can grow as long as a tree is high, and spread well beyond its crown. Use only a shrub-forming willow in a small garden.

The swamp cypress and dawn redwood are two other possibilities.

Shrubs
Bamboos: They make an interesting and arty type of hedge, but give them plenty of humus.

Dogwood: Particularly the scarlet, almost crimson Westonbirt variety.

Sea blackthorn: The female bush produces clusters of bright orange berries.

Guelder rose: There are few shrubs better suited to the autumnal garden. After flowering, its maple-shaped leaves colour brilliantly just as large bunches of glistening red berries appear.

Forget-me-not

Other plants. Irises, primulas, trollius, the mat-forming creeping Jenny, forget-me-nots, musk, the bog arum and giant

rhubarb all prefer to make their appearance in wet conditions. There is also a host of other flowers such as phlox and Michaelmas daisies.

Plants for gardens by the sea

Typical problems here are wind, and salt in the air which scorches the leaves of young plants. The first job is to erect a good wind barrier. This can be a plant enclosure:

Holm oak is good. In cold climates, the Japanese pine is better, but if the garden soil is alkaline the Austrian pine is best.

Trees. For planting as individual trees rather than as a tree barrier, the cedar. Leyland cypress, monkey puzzle, sycamore, white poplar and whitebeam are known for being salt-tolerant.

Shrubs. Olearias (daisy bushes) can be very effectively planted with mound-shaped hebes, contrasting in form. Hydrangeas grow well by the sea, and buddleia is surprisingly adaptable though it comes from deep in the interior of China. Bamboos like the moist air of coastal gardens, but they need some protection and are better not grown here as a hedge. Roses grow well too provided they are not subjected to high winds, particularly the white-flowering Scotch or Burnet rose that produces black hips in late summer, and the rugosa rose (see plants for dry soils).

Annuals, bulbs, and perennials. Annuals and bulbs like the loose, light soil that is fairly typical of coastal gardens. Among perennials, try lavender, scarlet lychnis and loosestrife. Finally, red hot pokers, carnations and pinks like living by the sea.

WHAT TO AVOID

Some plants can be more trouble than they are worth - roses, for instance, which get mildew, attract greenfly and need pruning. One exception is 'Zephirine Drouhin', a thornless, fragrant shrub rose in candy pink, which doesn't need pruning. Another is *Rosa* 'Rugosa' of which there are hybrids in white, rich crimson or that crude pink they use for Queen Alexandra's Rose Day; the flowers smell wonderful, flower for a long period (early summer until the frosts) and are virtually pest and disease free. Their only disadvantage (and it wouldn't be, for me) is that they are fairly tall bushes and two or three of them constitutes a complete rose garden.

A friend has sourly pointed out that my list of plants-not-to-be-bothered-with includes some of the most popular blooms in Britain, but more than popularity I am interested in ease, speedy results and no funereal tears.

You can't really expect any plants to survive young children or animals. Bashing or trampling, if it doesn't break a stem, will fracture or bruise the plant and may lead to a possible death from disease. Eating plants not intended for people will naturally disfigure them, and again this cannot be blamed on the plant, and some children or pets will eat anything.

You cannot use a small garden as a dog lavatory (even for small dogs) and expect anything to survive. Two labradors for a year left me with a bald lawn, two dying bay trees and a herbaceous border that looked like the Somme. Cats and kittens will be equally lethal.

Also to be avoided, if you or your friends have pets or small children, are *poisonous plants*. Small children can't understand why Mummy can pick the raspberries, but *they* aren't allowed to put the bright red yewberries in their mouths, and they don't realize that red laurel berries lead to collywobbles. Eating ivies, the *Hedera* species, can make you extremely ill, and mashed elderberries are a quick, violent emetic. Yew berries are poisonous, and stomach-upsetters include the barberries, *Berberis* species, and rowans, the *Sorbus* species. Euphorbias or spurges are to be treated with care, especially the so-called caper spurge - named not for its edibility but for its resemblence to caper buds. Rhubarb leaves are poisonous, laburnum seeds are *deadly* poisonous and so is almost any part of the Oleander, *Nerium oleander*, with pretty pink and white blossom that smells of vanilla: even brushing the leaves may convey upsetting poison to the mouth or hands of a child. Plants to send to those you hate include primulas, especially the pot-grown 'gift' types with hairy irritating leaves: they can give the recipient an allergic rash.

The Alexandra rose

Yewberries and Elderberries, pretty but poisonous.

Plants as temperamental and unreliable as a zoo panda's fertility period: plants which seem to grow vigorously, give a splendid display and then collapse, seemingly without reason or warning. Many large flowered clematis are so inclined, although species clematis are more reliable but have smaller flowers. Other too-tender plants, likely to go into decline for no apparent reason, are Californian lilacs (*Ceanothus* varieties). It is particularly important for the beginner gardener to avoid such plants as they will sap his self-confidence. In this context, lawns can be very delicate; quite apart from children and pets, diseases, weeds and moss are all likely to attack it; a lawn is considered by some to be the most time-consuming and accident-prone plant we grow. You have been warned.

Avoid plants that all flower at the same time of the year and leave you a boring garden for 9 months per annum. Most plants flower in summer; there are a few flowers which provide a brief spring splash - snowdrops, narcissi, daffodils, crocuses, bluebells - or an early spring flowering Oregon grape, the *Mahonia* species that is really easy to grow, and a few plants which can last on after summer, such as roses and buddleias. The flower season can be further extended by bulbs which flower in late autumn and winter - many crocuses, early irises, the heavily scented winter flowering shrub - winter sweet, *Chimonanthus praecox*. *Autumn colour* is easily extended by having a few of the small trees or shrubs whose foliage turns a brilliant colour at that time, or which become covered with brilliant berries. The elegant Japanese maples are hardy plants that give

coloured foliage; mountain ashes or rowan, the *Sorbus* species, may have startling, fiery leaves and brilliant berries, both in shades of red, orange, yellow, pink or white: these berries also provide a welcome feast to many birds in bad weather. And, of course, evergreens are green all the year round.

Plants that dislike your garden should not be allowed into it. For instance, bog plants only really like bog. In particular lime-haters are a problem in an alkaline-soil garden, unless no expense need be spared. It is possible inexpensively to lime an acid soil but very expensive to convert a limey soil with sequestering solutions or by replacing it with peat. Most rhododendrons, heaths and heather fall into this lime-hating category. Avoid wasted time, expense and misery by choosing only plants that suit your soil and climate.

Thorny plants can be a nuisance in a confined space or near paths. Some rose thorns nurse a diabolical devotion to the human flesh; the beautiful, old, delightfully scented 'Albertine' is one temptress to be avoided. Also beware of the hawthorn (*Crataegus* species), firethorn (*Pyracanth* species) and some barberries (*Berberis* species).

The invaders. Some plants seem to grow anywhere. Oh Good, you think at first, then Oh God, as they run rampant and start smothering everything in sight, including all the other plants and the greenhouse. Perhaps the most dangerous is the Russian vine, *Polygonum baldschuanicum*, or the silver lace vine, *P. aubertii* sometimes sold as the Russian vine. This is a plant recommended for covering unsightly sheds - it will, but may collapse them, too. The ivies, forms of the *Hedera* forms, are a better bet for covering purposes, but as ground cover, under trees, to cover bald patches or earth: however, they will charge along, scrambling through, up, and into almost anything. Avoid them, on walls with crumbling mortar, and unless you're prepared to cut them back several times a year.

Other ground cover plants that may be even greater menaces include the silver variegated dead nettle, *Lamiastrum galeobdolon* 'Variegatum'; it has pretty leaves and flowers but it will quickly climb through shrubs and small tress, edge into stone structures and insinuate itself, triffid-like, almost anywhere.

Ground cover plants which take a little longer to behave as badly are the periwinkles, *Vinca minor* and *V. major*.

Varieties of mint may be more trouble than they are worth, as they travel underground to appear elsewhere. Bamboos will often appear suddenly, shooting up well away from the tidy parent clump of which one is so proud.

However, all these plants are easy to control compared to the creeping thread speedwell, *Veronica filiformis*, a blue-eyed charmer that's sold to the innocent as a desirable rock plant; this prostrate creeper then shoots out in all directions before you've even seen its first flowers: and once in, it is almost impossible to eradicate. I have a friend whose lawn is blue in spring. I think it's lovely but he hates it. You have been warned.

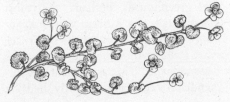

Some of the climber-rambler roses, such as 'New Dawn', are a seductive sight with pretty flowers and arching branches - but the arching branches will root and send up further loops: they can span 20 or 30 feet further, if allowed to. Once rooted all over the place, 'New Dawn' may be very difficult to eradicate because broken little bits of root send up shoots again and again. You'll be battling with it from 'New Dawn' to dusk.

A lively heath, *Erica carnea* 'Springwood White' may lie doggo for a year or two just gently increasing in girth, as so many do. Suddenly it can take off and move in all directions, even to the extent of smothering a few taller plants in the way of its expansion. 'Springwood Pink' is another similarly spreading heather.

Another quick spreader is *Meehania urticifolia*. This has scented lilac flowers, and pale green, heart shaped leaves, very pretty, but beware! This plant almost *runs* and will travel yards in a year, scrambling ruthlessly through shrubs and other plants to do so.

So think twice before ordering quick spreaders: you don't want to spend your spare time battling with the invaders.

CHOOSING TREES AND SHRUBS

A tree is a beautiful thing, but you may not live long enough either to see its full beauty or to realize what a mistake you made in planting a forest tree in a suburban garden. By all means if you have room, and concern for future generations, plant oaks, beeches, limes, copper beech, sycamores, cypresses and cedars. But there are others which are more likely to fit the scale of the average garden.

Before you buy a tree, sit down with a rough plan of your garden and work out where it will cast shade, when it has grown to a respectable size. Because somebody *hadn't* bothered to think about this, I once inherited a garden that got practically no sunlight, and was in constant gloom. I consequently developed a feverish interest in shade ground cover. Very little will grow under most trees, besides spring bulbs when there's no foliage overhead, but for the rest of the year you've lost that bit of garden.

Among those you might consider are such *flowering trees* as: magnolia, hawthorn, laburnun (this is poisonous, see poison section), and flowering almond, cherry, apple and plum.

There are also *trees with eye-catching bark* or brilliant foliage: mountain ash, silver birch and maple.

If you buy them through mail-order they will probably have no soil around the roots. Instead they will be wrapped in moist sphagnum moss and sealed in a polythene bag. If you buy a plant from a local nursery, it may come with a ball of its native earth around the roots, wrapped in sacking. Small rare shrubs are often planted without removing the sacking which soon rots, but remove the wrapping from larger shrubs and trees

so that the roots can be carefully spread out during planting.

Most garden centres specialize in container-plant trees and shrubs, which being established in pots suffer minimum disturbance when moved. These can be put in a garden at almost any time in almost any place: all you do is dig a hole, put the tree and container in the hole, water it in well and then keep it moist but not soggy with regular watering. However, for real sons of the soil, here is....

How to plant a tree

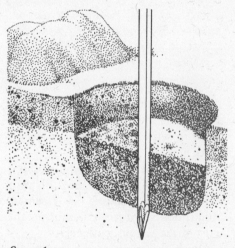

Stage 1

Before you unwrap the tree or shrub dig a hole. Make it wide and deep enough to take the spread of the roots. Remove the *topsoil* and put it in a heap. Loosen the soil at bottom of the hole with fork or pick, and fork in compost, peat or leaf mould (mixed with the topsoil).

Then drive in a stout stake at the centre of the hole as if at a vampire's heart. Plant the tree no deeper than it was in the nursery - you'll see the mark.

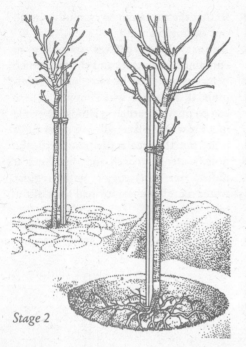

Stage 2

Daphne. Star shaped, wonderfully fragrant flowers, white to blush pink. Some species are poisonous.

Deutzia. A fountain of white flowers in late spring, but attractive all year round.

There are three others which *must* have acid soil:

Kalmia. (Mountain Laurel). Evergreen, with white, pink-tinged flowers in late spring.

Azalea. So many dazzling varieties from white to yellow to peach to scarlet.

Rhododendron. Hybrid evergreen. Magnificent white, pink, rose, scarlet, dark red, mauve or lavender blooms. You can really get hooked on rhododendrons.

Spread out the roots, then shovel back the soil over them. Shake the tree up and down to settle the soil in between the roots.

Stand on the loose soil and stomp it down HARD with the heel of your wellies. Firm planting is essential. Muddy boots, not green thumbs, are the signs of the serious gardener.

Attach the trunk of the tree to the stake with some soft material, such as a laddered pair of tights or 4 inch wide strips of plastic covering, cut from a carrier bag.

Ornamental shrubs are a safe bet and need less looking after than flowers. Some of the best are tough enough to withstand just about any British soil or weather. Buddleias, cotoneaster, forsythia, hydrangea, lilac and viburnun have already been recommended and to these can be added:

The best time to plant most trees or shrubs is in early autumn when the ground is still warm and the roots have a chance to settle in before winter does. The next best time is in *early* spring, as soon as the ground is workable. (at either time the plant is *dormant*, not growing).

Evergreens should be planted in very late summer or very late spring.

Buying

Before buying trees or shrubs, scout any garden centre that specializes in good stock. The good ones have acres of well-tended baby trees, of every age and variety suited to local growing conditions. If there isn't a good source of supply in your neighbourhood, or if you haven't the time to visit one, you can safely order trees and shrubs from a reliable grower by catalogue (see page 112).

HOW TO MULTIPLY YOUR PLANTS

Once your garden is established, it costs very little to multiply the plants in it and also to grow potted presents for other people. Giving and receiving cuttings from friends is a very pleasant procedure: every time I tend a gift plant I remember the donor with pleasure. So here are the simple procedures to multiply your plants: I have not included the difficult methods of layering, grafting and budding.

GROWING PLANTS FROM SEED

For those who think that growing plants from seed is going to be fun, and well worth the trouble, here's the trouble you have to take, outlined in gruesome detail.

What to choose

You can propagate from seed saved from your own garden, but the off-spring may be inferior without controlled pollination. The advantage of buying seed from reputable seedsmen is the variety of choice and the health and vigour of the resulting plants.

Garden centres and shops provide a pretty good selection of seeds, while the illustrated catalogues available from the leading specialist seed houses offer a choice that's truly mouthwatering.

Choose hardy plants which grow quickly: the more delicate or long-term plants are not for the beginner, however pretty they may look on the packet. Beginners should try to restrict themselves to a half-dozen or so different kinds - that way, there's more chance to learn about the habits and needs of individual types than if you rush around trying looking after dozens of unfamiliar species at the same time.

How to sow seed outdoors

Many seeds can be sown directly in a sunny part of the garden (mark the place by spearing the packet on a stick) where you want them to grow but other seeds must be germinated carefully in a special seed mixture and then potted when they're large enough to leave the incubator. Whichever they are always buy *fresh* seed from a reputable salesman. It's really well worth buying F1 hybrid seeds, which are more expensive, but they produce strong plants with larger flowers and are more resistant to disease than ordinary varieties. This does not apply to vegetables, where the strict uniformity of F1 seed will produce all your veggies to harvest on the same day.

Sow seeds in mid-spring. Try to avoid sowing seeds in wet weather, or cold, wet soil. Wait.

At the beginning of spring, when it's bearable to go out, pick your spot and fork it over lightly, scattering one bucketful of sedge peat and 3 oz. of fish fertilizer to the square yard. If you can't get fish fertilizer, use Fison's GROW-MORE. At mid spring, when the world is warming up and the soil is reasonably dry, rake it over and sow the seed in patches (not in rows; only corporation gardeners do that).

Scatter seeds thinly over evenly raked soil or in a shallow trench, about ½ inch deep for small seeds, 1 inch for large seeds. You can make a row of holes with your finger or form a trench with a hoe or by pulling an upended broom handle along the ground. Sow seeds, then rake the soil back and firm with back of rake or tap firmly with your boot.

If you want to show off, you can make a pattern in the ground with a stick, then sow different colours in each patch you have made. Hence Prince of Wales feathers, municipal clocks and your loved one's initials. (Easier to remove than tatoos, should you change the loved one.)

There is always an element of chance in sowing seeds. Some 'take', some don't. So you always sow more than you need, and they are thinned out as they grow. Thinning out is merely removing the surplus, weakest, smallest, straggly seedlings which leaves room for the others to grow 1 or 2 inches apart.

When the seedlings have grown to about 2 inches high, thin them out again so that they have room to grow. How far apart they should be depends on the flower - a couple of inches for alyssum or 15 inches for sunflowers (it will say on the packet).

Until the plants are established weed the bed by hand, not with a hoe (because you may disturb the plant roots or even chop them off); this is a fiddling job. Snip dead flower heads off, to encourage others to flower and keep well watered.

Annuals

Annuals have only one growing cycle - they die within the year. They can provide a beautiful blaze of colour in the garden (often when you are away on holiday).

Nevertheless annuals are exceedingly good value for money. For a few pence and a very little effort you can have some really wonderful flowers in all colours, shapes and sizes. If you sow the seeds outdoors in mid-spring, they should begin to flower in early summer and, depending on the variety, go on until autumn. Early in that season you can sow those varieties which are hardy enough to withstand winter weather when small, and these will start to flower from late spring. There is a list of annuals that you may feel you can't live without on page 30.

Unless you live in a really warm climate, only *hardy* annuals can be sown directly into the ground. *Half-hardy* annuals (they are marked on the list) will not survive frost. They have to be weaned from seed in a greenhouse or propagating case that can be set to provide the ideal temperature for germination. Usually this is in the region of 65-70°F, but there will be instructions on the seed packets.

All fine seed is best germinated in a propagating case before planting out in early summer, but depending on the temperature quoted on the seed packet you may be able to create suitable conditions elsewhere.

Growing from seed indoors

Get a seed box or a flowerpot. It must have drainage holes. Wash well.

Fill with a peat-based seeding compost, such as LEVINGTON SOWING AND CUTTING COMPOST. Firm down gently with fingertips (don't pack hard). Water the compost and allow to drain overnight before sowing.

Sow seeds thinly and evenly: cover large seeds with a thin layer of seed compost. Leave small seeds as they fall.

Cover *seed tray* with a sheet of glass to retain moisture; wipe glass daily to remove condensation. Keep at temperature of about 60°F in the shade. Cover the glass with newspaper until seedlings appear, then allow full light, but not direct sunlight. Remove the glass as soon as you see shoots, before your seedlings get leggy.

Keep the seed compost moist.

You can sow *seeds in a flowerpot* and turn it into a greenhouse by putting a big polythene bag over it, held in place with a rubber band. As soon as seedlings appear, put flowerpot in full light (but not direct sunlight) and remove the bag a few days later. To prevent uneven growth, turn the pot round a bit every day. Keep the seed compost moist.

Pricking out

When seedlings are big enough to handle without damage (about ½ inch) they should be pricked out into seed boxes or pots, where they will have more room to grow. A suitable compost is JOHN INNES NO. 1.

Hold the leaf carefully, because the stem is easily crushed. Gently uproot the seedlings and replant in holes made with a blunt-ended instrument, such as a pencil or your finger. Make the hole big enough, so that it won't cramp the root. Plant the seeds 1½ inches apart, water well to settle them in and keep them in the shade for a couple of days.

Then grow the seedlings in light and warmth until they are sturdy.

Hardening Off. After the seedlings have recovered from pricking out, they have gradually to get used to tougher conditions until they can be planted outdoors. Move them to a cooler place before putting them outdoors.

Town gardens hardly allow space for a greenhouse, but you can do a lot with a frame, which is a kind of miniature greenhouse. Make your own out of a discarded window put on top of three rows of bricks to form a rectangle. Instead of a window, you can tack clear plastic heavyweight (500 gauge) sheet to a plywood frame. Put pots and seed-boxes underneath it and keep the frame slightly open for ventilation. But beware of late frosts.

Biennials

Biennials, too, are seed grown. Most of the cottage-garden flowers - Canterbury bells, wallflowers, foxgloves, Sweet Williams and hollyhocks, for example - come under this category. In theory they are sown outdoors in late spring and will start to produce leaves in the summer, but will not flower until the spring or summer of the following year. In practice, if you sow them in early summer many will flower the following spring.

More time-consuming than annuals, most have to be sown in a seed bed, thinned, and in autumn planted out. Some need stopping (the growing tip is broken off when they are about 4in tall) to make side-shoots grow lower down and thus carry more flowers.

Perennials

Herbaceous perennials - ornamental plants like delphiniums, lupins, poppies and red-hot pokers - can be grown from seed and go on flowering for years. The disadvantages are that they don't usually flower until at least a year after sowing, and they need to be started in a nursery bed and then transplanted to where you want them to flower. For a beginner, I don't think they're worth the trouble - you can usually buy the young plants locally in spring, and the specialist nurseries will send them mail-order.

Vegetables

Most vegetables are seed-grown every year. Some take up too much space in small gardens: the principal offenders are the cabbage family, including Brussels sprouts and sprouting broccoli. Some vegetables need lots of warmth - tomatoes, sweet peppers and aubergines, for example - while others, such as cauliflowers, are temperamental. Growing onions is a particularly fiddly business.

As ye sow, so ye want to reap, not weep, so avoid these and concentrate instead on easy-to-grow vegetables that won't take up much of your time. These include lettuce, courgettes, broad beans (the dwarfer kinds such as 'The Sutton' and 'The Midget'), runner beans and spinach. There are also the sunny-tempered root vegetables such as parsnips, carrots, beetroot, turnips and radishes. Some of these veggies, sown in the spring, will be ready to eat in summer or autumn; one or two can be sown in summer to be picked in winter. Follow the instructions on the packets.

Herbs

A lot of herbs can be grown from seed sown outdoors in spring. Some of the easiest are the annuals: dill, coriander, fennel and borage, and the perennials: marjoram, chives and angelica. Parsley is supposed to be difficult, but the secret of good, quick growth is warm soil. Sow the seed outdoors at any time from mid-spring to mid-summer and it will germinate in seven to fourteen days, instead of the four or five weeks if sown earlier in the year when the soil is cold. If you sow one batch in mid-spring and another in mid-summer, you will have fresh parsley continuously available throughout the year. In the second year it will flower and seed itself.

CUTTINGS

A cutting is a small piece of the stem of the plant with a healthy looking shoot sprouting from it. When the shoot is stuck in soil or (if soft stemmed) in water it grows roots.

Once you have bought your basic purchase of potting compost and hormone rooting powder, for absolutely no money at all and hardly any effort you can multiply almost everything in your garden.

Take *soft stem cuttings* in early spring (that includes house plants and cacti) when the strong growth starts; pelargoniums (geraniums) and fuchsias can be propagated up to late summer.

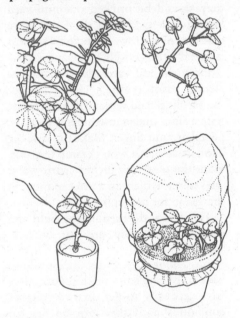

Take a sharp knife and cut the tips off young healthy shoots, about 2 - 4 inches long. They should have about 4 nodes (leaf joints). Cut the stem *straight across* just below a node, and pinch-off or cut-off (*never* pull-off) the leaves at this bottom node. Better to use shoots without flower buds as roots are unlikely to form if buds or flowers are already present. Dip in rooting powder (try SERADIX).

Fill a small pot with LEVINGTON SOWING AND CUTTING COMPOST to about ½ inch from the top:

firm it down with your fingertips. One pot will take several cuttings. Insert the cuttings, to about one third of their length, close to the rim of the pot. Water well which will have the effect of settling the cuttings in. Put a polythene bag (big enough not to touch the leaves) over the pot and secure it round the pot with one of the elastic bands that you have been collecting from the postman. The polythene bag forms its own little terrarium, which provides warmth and moisture which is essential while the cutting has no roots. Do not remove it to let the moisture out. Stand pot in good light but no sunshine until new leaves appear.

When the cuttings are growing, transplant them into small pots of proper potting mixture, such as LEVINGTON COMPOST. If you use peat pots (like ROOT O POTS) there's no need to disturb the roots by transplanting again, so I recommend them. You just shove the peat pot into the garden soil and eventually the roots grow through the peat and into the soil.

Outdoor cuttings (for propagating shrubs, fruit bushes - but not blackcurrants and rambler roses): In September, pull off a sideshoot about 12 inches long, from low down on the stem. Remove leaves and buds from bottom 4 inches.

Dig a narrow 6-inch trench in a shady part of the garden. Sprinkle sharp sand in the bottom. Stand the 'heel' or base of the cutting on the sand and replace soil: firm it down, water well and leave for a year.

DIVISION

This procedure defies mathematics, because the result of division is multiplication.

Bulbs increase by producing side-shoots or bulblets. Remove these when the leaves have dried, then plant outside to grow into full-sized bulbs.

Perennials that grow in clumps, such as violets, primroses, and primulas, aren't propagated by cuttings but by carefully dividing the roots into several smaller clumps. Do this gently by hand, as if you were dealing with tangled hair.

If this isn't possible, cut through the clump with a sharp knife. Make sure that there is some top growth in each clump. Pot each bit separately in LEVINGTON COMPOST.

For larger perennial clumps, gently pull the roots apart with two forks. Discard the old, woody central part. Replant the outside shoots separately in late autumn or early spring.

GRASS AND HOW TO GROW IT

Grass is a nuisance: a lawn is *un*natural, so raising one is full of problems and can grow into a lifetime fixation.

Thick, thick books have been written about grass and how to grow it. Charts that look like a railway timetable have been drawn-up as annual lawn guides. A lawn is a very complex subject if you cover all lawn treatments (mowing: spiking: rolling: watering: feeding: dressing: weeding - by hand is essential) and all lawn troubles (to name but a few - weeds, including dandelions, daisies and clover: moss: lichen: algae: anthills: pearlwort: earthworms: moles: leatherjackets: crane flies: ants: wire worms: fungus: snowmould: fairy rings and red thread).

However, I assume that you are after a pretty patch of green grass in which you can stretch out comfortably, rather than the perfect bowling green.

It took me 10 years to realize that what I had to do with my lawn in order to achieve my very low aim was to find out what it did *naturally* and then improve it a bit and be happy with the result. After all, grass is only one part of a garden and it should tone in colour with the surrounding countryside, not stick out like a sore, bright green thumb.

Don't worry about the condition of your neighbour's lawn: remember that the grass is *always* greener on the other side of the fence.

Don't worry if the sun bakes the grass brown: as soon as the rain returns, so will most of the grass, and in the meantime the brown no doubt tones in with the surrounding countryside. And if the surrounding countryside consists of slabs of concrete, then brown will tone in just as well as grass.

Don't worry about weeds during the growing season. I long ago decided that a perfect lawn is unnecessary, unnatural, impractical and too much trouble. I like daisies and dandelions and buttercups. And weeds are cut down to size when the grass is cut.

Don't worry if your lawn isn't billiard-table level: a gentle slope, or irregular slope can look charming, but you don't want a *lumpy* lawn because it's impossible to mow.

But a lawn needs light, sun and air: don't try to raise a lawn in heavy shade (look for suitable, alternative ground cover).

There are two ways of establishing a lawn 1. the cheap, long one - by sowing seed 2. the expensive, instant method - by laying turves.

Once your lawn is established, *pick your mower* with care: an electric rotary mower that collects grass.

Always cut the grass when it is long enough but never let it get too high. This probably means once a week from early spring to late autumn.

Don't mow too soon or too close, because you might damage the lawn.

Feeding the lawn: 1st feeding in mid-spring. Use general purpose lawn fertilizer with plenty of nitrogen for green growth.

2nd feeding in early summer, to keep grass growing the rest of the summer.

3rd feeding in mid-autumn. Choose an autumn lawn fertilizer with a high proportion of phosphate to feed the roots and not much nitrogen.

Apply fertilizer in showery weather, so the fertilizer is washed into the soil: if it doesn't rain within 2 days, then water it in. Always apply fertilizer evenly, to avoid grass scorch and uneven growth.

SOWING GRASS SEED

Advantages:
*Cheapest method of creating a lawn.

*From a *reliable* supplier it's possible to acquire just the right mix to suit your shady/sunny/partly shaded/excessively wet garden conditions.

*You begin with a weedless lawn.

Disadvantages:
*Thorough preparation of seed bed vital.

*Grass seedlings are easy prey to birds and bad weather.

*Takes time (at least 9 months) before lawn is ready to use.

If you want to sow your lawn, your local garden centre (or see the Direct Mail list) will offer different seeds for different soils and purposes. There are different mixtures for:

A lawn in the sun (Suttons "SUMMER DAY" grass seed)

A lawn in the shade (Suttons "GREEN GLADE" grass seed)

A hardwearing lawn to withstand dogs or children (Suttons "SUMMER PLAY" grass seed).

The best all-purpose mixture is the seed sold as "SHADY LAWN", which is fairly drought-resistant, and long-lasting.

The best time to sow is at the end of summer or early autumn. Remember that seeds like a warm, moist soil in which to grow.

You'll hear that spring is also a grass sowing time, but growth may be slow if the winter has been bad and the soil hasn't had a chance to warm up. Also, spring-sown lawns rarely tolerate children's playtime during the summer of the same year.

Preparing the ground

Preparing the site

1. Remove weeds, rubble and rubbish.

2. Stack the topsoil on one side. Topsoil is your precious top layer of soil (generally darker than the subsoil beneath) which contains all the nutrition that plants (and grass seed) need to grow. Protect it at all costs. If it is less than 6 inches deep, buy extra. When you stack topsoil, make sure the piles are not too high or the structural quality of the topsoil (important for the soil to breathe and drain properly) will be ruined.

3. Now grade the ground, if you want a sloping or a level lawn and don't have a suitable base. This is a process called 'cut-and-fill'.

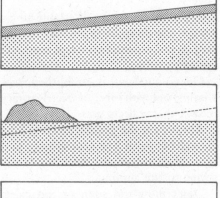
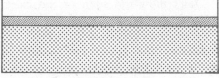

Remove topsoil before levelling a slope

4. Dig the site over with fork, spade or mechanical cultivator to a depth of about 9 inches. Be sure to break up any clods. Remove all weeds.

5. If you have a sticky, dense, clay-type soil, work in some coarse grit (builder's merchants supply it) to help drainage. Every time you turn the soil over with your spade, work the grit into it at a rate

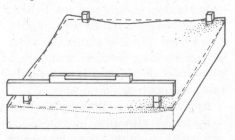
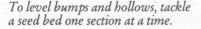

To level bumps and hollows, tackle a seed bed one section at a time.

70

Preparing a seed bed

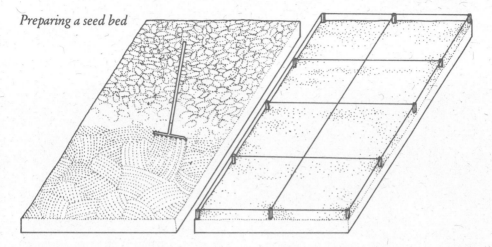

of about 2 lbs to the square yard. Don't overdo it. Peat, compost, Perlite, Vermiculite and Hortag are also effective for this problem. If you use compost, make sure it is well decomposed, or it will rob the soil of nitrogen (essential to healthy, *green* grass).

6. Replace the topsoil.

7. Create a fine seed bed by working the soil over with a rake, treading the soil between rakings.

Repeat the process until the bumps and hollows disappear, the soil feels fine and crumbly, and the bed is firm enough not to show heel marks.

To ensure a really level bed, concentrate on 6 foot square sections of the bed at a time. Drive pegs into the 4 corners of the square, having first marked each peg to a consistent depth. With a spirit level check that the pegs are level. Redistribute the soil within the square so that the bed level coincides with the marks on the pegs.

Sowing seed

Seeds need oxygen, heat and moisture to germinate. Careful preparation of the seed bed looks after the first requisite. Sowing at the correct time (see above) looks after the second; you must also make sure that there is sufficient moisture in the right places. The ideal sowing medium is a bed that is dry on the surface and moist beneath: too much water rots the seeds, so pick your sowing day carefully. Generally the best seed distribution rate is 1½ oz per square yard. Having worked out how much seed you will need for your lawn, divide it into four equal parts, distributing each part uniformly. If the bed is large, it's a good idea to divide it up with sticks and string and sow each section individually.

Rake lightly over the site to cover the seed. Do *not* cover the seed too well.

In ideal conditions, the seeds will germinate within 14 days. Let it grow to a height of at least 2 inches before giving it its first mowing with a mower set to 1 inch. This light cutting encourages the seedlings to produce side shoots, helping to form a dense turf.

Keep the new lawn well watered; you'll have less of a problem in this respect if you sow in early autumn.

71

Thick, thick books have been written about grass and how to grow it. It took me 10 years to realize that what I had to do with my lawn in order to achieve my very low aim was to find out what it did naturally, improve it a bit and be happy with the result.

Carole Latimer

I prefer to see nodding buttercups and daisies amidst any green I grow; the graceful dandelion, with its all too short season . . .

Neil Holmes

Neil Holmes

In a really small town garden, an area of grass will fast get trodden to death. You could lay concrete tiles in natural, terra cotta or slate colouring, or terrazzo.

Problem conditions
See p.53, a what-to-plant guide. Dry shade is created by thirsty, full-leaved trees and hedges that take enormous amounts of moisture from the soil and create severe planting problems beneath.

Michael Warren

When I first had a garden, everything died because I just kept trying to grow what I liked, oblivious of the garden's soil and light. You really have to choose the plants to fit the garden.
Heather and dwarf conifers are well-suited to an acid soil.

Anthony Huxley

The easiest way to a small pool is to use a tank or barrel (I've used an old porcelain sink) and sink it into the ground.

Jerry Harpur

Water has a fascinating, forbidden magic: a pool in your garden can be delightfully glamorous if it's well-sited, properly made and well stocked with goldfish. See p.78.

LAYING TURF

Advantages

*The quickest method; an instant lawn.

*No need to prepare topsoil to a fine seedbed.

*You lay turf in autumn or winter when there's little else to do in the garden.

Disadvantages

*Turf, compared to seed, is expensive.

*In a terrace of houses you may have to drag it through the house to the garden.

*In England (though not in America where turf is big business) luxury grade turf is hard to find.

How to lay turf

Prepare ground as for seeding, though final seedbed need not be as fine.

Cut the turves into manageable sizes.

Check turves are of uniform thickness otherwise all your efforts to create a level surface will be wasted. Turf thickness is traditionally controlled by a process called boxing.

Place the turf, grass down into an open-ended box

Remove excess earth with sharp tool (a drawknife as shown is best, but even a light spade would do).

Inspect each turf and pull out any weeds. Put poor turves on one side and only use if necessary.

The right way to lay turf is to
1. work in straight lines;

2. begin from one side of the site;

3. lay a plank on top of the first line when laying the second. *Never stand on the soil bed* beyond the turf or directly on the turf;

4. lay the turves tightly together and stagger them in each line (like bricks in a wall) to help bonding.

Finally, treat your turf to a liberal sprinkling of a mix made of peat, sand and a little fertilizer; brush it into any cracks between turves. Water turves well if the weather is dry. A few days later, give your new lawn a *light* rolling, just enough to settle the turves; do *not* try to flatten any unfortunate hillocks or you will damage the grass.

73

THE BASIC PRINCIPLES OF WATERING

This is far more important than ever you thought: a token dribble, a guilty flood on parched dry leaves or a hoseblast at dusk is not good enough.

Water indoors.......

In winter: in the morning.

In summer: anytime, but always give the plants a good long slow drink.

Over-enthusiastic *watering* will only raise the mortality rate: overwatering is the most common cause of indoor plant death.

Air is needed by roots, so the potting mixture should be moist, not boggy. Feel the mixture with your fingers and water only if it's barely moist. Never leave plants standing in saucers of water.

A plant should never dry out: if it wilts, you've neglected or over-indulged it with criminal results. Your eyes can (eventually instinctively) tell you what a plant needs: if you talk to your plants, the neighbours might think you're gaga but *you* will notice the condition of your plants.

Water outdoors.....

In spring and autumn: The danger here is early or late winter frosts. It is unlikely that much watering will be necessary, but avoid doing it in the morning because it might be too cold, and water will lower the temperature still further.

In summer: in the morning or the evening.

Never water in full sun, because (1) hot sun evaporates the water, (2) water could act as a magnifying glass and scorch the leaves of the plant.

If possible, use a sprinkler with a fine spray: a cheap sprinkler is better than a brutal hosing or downpour from a watering can, most of which ends in the drain not the soil.

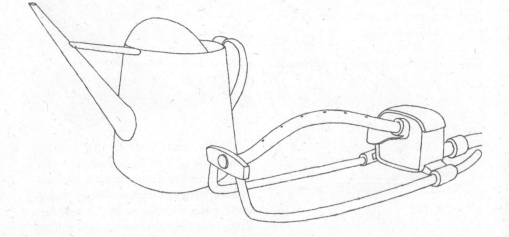

PRUNING

Pruning needs to be tackled with great skill and care. As with watering, too little is safer than too much. If you are a newcomer to the art, my advice is to watch an expert at work. Since not all plants are pruned in the same way, or at the same time, you will pick up some useful tips and learn to avoid the potentially deadly pitfalls. You should avoid the plants which need heavy and regular pruning entirely, until you've had time to learn how to deal with the problem. And don't buy any tree or shrub until it's at least three years old, by which time the nurseryman will have done the all-important basic shaping for you.

There are three main reasons for pruning: to train a plant into a more pleasing shape, to encourage it to produce new growth, and to get rid of surplus or decayed wood so that sunlight and air can reach the remaining parts and thus improve the plant's general health. If you leave a plant unpruned it will not only start to look bedraggled, but will become so drained of energy that it will produce few flowers and fruit in later years.

Pruning and growth

Pruning doesn't stop growth - it encourages it, but in a different part of the plant. Plants respond differently to the various ways of pruning, whose timing and severity also has an effect on the vigour of the new growth. If you cut out the main growing point you make the plant put out new shoots. If you cut back the new growth of lateral shoots (soft-wood pruning), two or more new shoots will start to grow where only one grew before. This is the kind of pruning that a plant needs once it has become established, in order to improve its fruiting or flowering capabilities.

Hard-wood pruning is the most severe form. It involves cutting right back into the old part of the stems - in other words, removing any branches which have already borne fruit or flowers. The purpose of this drastic action is to wake up the dormant buds under the older bark and make them put out new growth at a rate of knots. Neglected shrubs often need this treatment to pull them back into shape. Don't worry if they look rather sorry for themselves for some time afterwards. The important thing is to get rid of all the decayed, diseased or tangled wood by cutting right back to clean, healthy growth.

Some plants produce their flowers on top of the previous season's growth, while with others the buds are produced on short spurs which develop on wood that is over one year old. Each needs different treatment so that the plant will continue to flourish in its next growth cycle. Here's a table showing you when and how to tackle most of the major categories of trees and shrubs:

Type	When to prune	Technique
Apples, pears (tip-bearing)	Winter	Removed damaged and tangled branches
Apples, pears (spur-bearing)	Winter	Cut back leader branches to ⅔ their original length. Trim lateral branches to last 4-5 healthy buds
Peach, plum, cherry	Summer	Remove damaged and tangled branches while tree is still in full leaf; after fruiting
Raspberry, blackberry	Directly after picking	Remove fruit-bearing wood, but leave healthiest new shoots
Blackcurrant	Directly after picking	Remove 2 or 3 old branches completely. Shorten remainder down to strong new lateral branches
Gooseberry, redcurrant	Winter	Remove tangled growth in centre of plant and snip off tips of some of remaining branches
Roses (bush, climbing)	Early spring	Remove the weak and straggling shoots first and cut back remainder by up to ⅓
Roses (rambler)	Directly after flowering	Cut away all flower-bearing stems
Evergreens	Early spring	Remove damaged and tangled branches
Conifers	Late summer	Remove damaged and tangled branches
Shrubs (Spring-flowering)	Directly after flowering	For those which flower on wood one or more years old, remove dead wood and shorten flower-bearing stems to wood of current year. For those flowering on current year's growth, cut back hard to old wood.

76

Shrubs (Early- mid summer flowering)	Directly after flowering	Remove shoots which have flowered, cutting back to strong new laterals.
Shrubs (summer/ autumn flowering)	Early spring	Remove old wood not carrying much new growth, the weakest shoots of the new growth; and old flowered growth.

Remember not to prune newly planted fruit trees until their second winter. Later, as the plant begins to establish itself, concentrate on improving its shape. Bush and cane fruits are cut down rather hard as soon as they are planted: to within 4 - 9in of the soil depending on the variety. This will encourage strong new growth.

You can tackle most pruning jobs with a good, sharp pair of secateurs. For trees, a small hand-saw will be useful (special pruning saws are available). If you're thinning out dead or congested growth you should cut off branches flush with the main stem. Do this first, before tackling the new growth. This can be cut back by making cuts no more than ⅛in above the bud, downwards

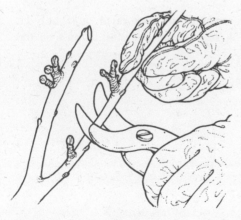

The correct way to prune

and away from it. Never cut down towards the bud, because this will direct rainwater on to it and cause rotting. Cut cleanly so that there are no jagged edges which will expose the stem to further splitting, damage and disease. Sealants are available to coat cuts made in thick, woody stems or branches over ½ in and protect the wood from rotting.

Preventing invasions

You'll need to keep an eye on vigorously growing shrubs and climbers to make sure they stay where they're meant to be. Cut back shoots and stems on the outsides of the plants with your secateurs, making the cuts just above the leaf joints. If the centres of the plants are turning into miniature jungles, cut away enough stems and branches so that the rest can spread out to their full size and enjoy their full share of light and air. Do this about once a month, depending on how quickly the plant grows.

Never be tempted to cut off the top of a tree just to make it look neater. It will simply stop growing. On the other hand there may be occasions when you have to do precisely this. It has just taken me a year to get the tree surgeon to come round and saw down a bay tree that was five feet high ten years ago and is now three stories high and blocking the backs of three entire buildings.

A GARDEN POOL

Water has a fascinating, forbidden magic: a pool in your garden can be delightfully glamorous if it's well-sited, properly made and well stocked with lilies and goldfish: it can be a horrible midge ridden headache if it isn't.

What sort of pool do you want?

The easiest way.... to a small pool is to use a tank or barrel (I've used an old porcelain sink) and sink it into the ground. But even a small pool such as this is a potential danger if you have children under 10 years old in your garden.

Small formal pools look fine on a raised patio, or other paved area. They can be made from a tank or half barrel, sunk to its rim in the ground with paving protruding an inch or so over the end to camouflage the rim. Alternatively, a section of concrete sewer pipe can be sunk in similar fashion with a concrete floor added and painted with bitumen to seal the join.

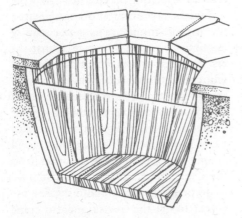

The informal pool

The simplest way to make a small pool is to line it with PVC or butyl rubber sheeting, which will stand up to the pressure and are easy to move if you want to change your pond. AVOID... ready-formed artificial pools made from plastic or fibreglass, they're easy to install if they're small, but they will continue to look highly artificial. Concrete-lined pools are fine, but it's a hard skilled job to construct one. A puddled clay pond is also a skilled task.

Plan your pool

What will it cost? As so often, the answer is that it depends on the size of your pool: the size of the liner: paving for the edges: sand: rocks: plants. A telephone enquiry to your local garden centre should give you the answer.

Pool position. Water plants need the sun. Rotting leaves can pollute a pool, stink abominably and kill the fish, so site your plant in the open, not under or too close to trees.

The lowest level of your garden (where nature would put it) is probably the best site.

Make sure your pool is within hose - length, in order to fill it, and refill after cleaning every few years.

Shape, size and depth. A wobbly fat kidney shape is easiest. Don't be too

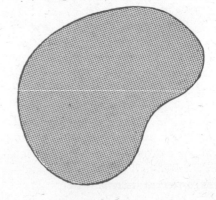

ambitious with the shape or you'll have problems with the sheeting liner.

The pool should be designed to take a standard size sheet of butyl rubber otherwise you'll have a tricky join. You can have a few small goldfish in a 3 foot by 3 foot pool but larger fish need at least a 9-foot length.

Very shallow pools can freeze solid in winter, killing fish. Avoid this with a depth of 15 inches or more. And then it's deep enough to grow a few aristocratic water lilies.

Plan some kind of paving round the sides of the pool, to stand on in safety and to avoid lawn mowings or flower bed earth getting in the pool. It is then easy to look after plants and inspect your pond life.

The size of the liner. No matter what shape you decide on, the size of the liner will be X long by Y wide. No overlap for edges is required; the elasticity of the material allows for this.

X = length of pool + depth + depth again

Y = width of pool + depth + depth again.

Example: a 4 foot x 3 foot pool, 2 foot deep would be:

$$X = 4' + 2' + 2' = 8'$$
$$Y = 3' + 2' + 2' = 7'$$

So you would need, for this example, a sheet of butyl rubber measuring 8 foot x 7 foot.

Don't economize by using thin polythene sheeting, which can be punctured by garden tools, birds' beaks and children poking with sticks. Special reinforced sheeting made specifically for pools is better, but best of all is butyl rubber sheeting. It is certainly the most expensive but if you are having a pool it is silly to cut corners here.

Plants in plastic containers

There are special plastic containers for pond plants with open mesh sides. Line them with an old bit of rag or sacking, fill with a mixture of good topsoil and compost, put in the plant and then cover the surface of the compost with stones to stop it washing away. Lower gently into the pool.

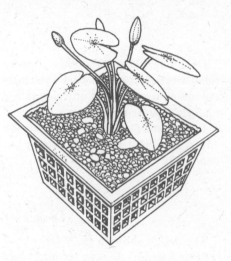

Plastic containers allow the plant to be moved around, they allow you to take the plant out of the pond to divide it up if necessary and they make cleaning out the pool that much easier if it ever has to be done. Many plants are happy in about 6 inches of water. Some prefer more and some less. For those that prefer less it is quite simple to put a brick under the container to raise it up.

How to make your pool

Having planned your pool on graph paper, peg it out with string on the garden site you have chosen. Decide where you will put the soil that you excavate.

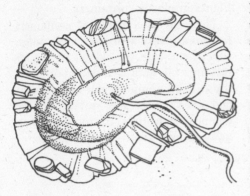

Remove all sharp stones, firm the earth, then cover it with a 1-inch layer of soft sand, to give a smooth bed for the liner to lay on.

Carefully position the liner over the pool, so that there is an equal overlap all round. Weigh down the edges with bricks.

Fill the pool from a hose. As you do so, the weight of the water will pull the liner and bricks in towards the pool, firmly and gently moulding the liner in position.

Dig, Dig, Dig. Smoothly sloping sides are necessary so that in winter expanding ice will slide upwards rather than exert pressure sideways.

Leave some shallow areas at the edges, in which to stand water plant containers.

Cut off the surplus liner, leaving about a 6-inch wide overlap of liner all round. Tuck this flat against the earth and pave over it.

Design for a simple pool

The design shows a fairly large pool (12 foot x 9 foot) that can accommodate a lot of plants. You can easily scale it down or up.

There are shelves for marginal plants that need shallow water and also areas where you can get right to the water's edge to feed the fish or peer into the depths to check whether there still are any.

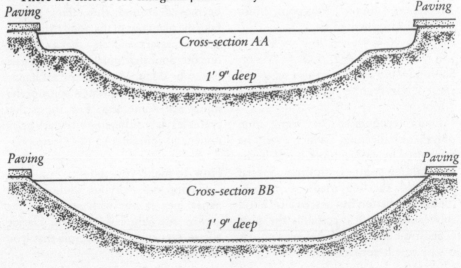

Paving

Cross-section AA

1' 9" deep

Paving

Paving

Cross-section BB

1' 9" deep

Paving

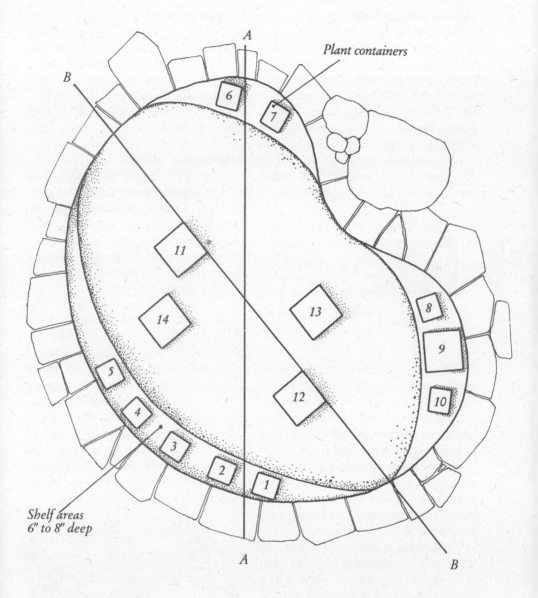

A

Plant containers

B

6

7

11

14

13

8

9

5

10

4

3

12

2

1

*Shelf areas
6" to 8" deep*

A

B

1. Pontederia cordata
2. Lythrum salicaria & Iris Atea
3. Iris pseudacorus variegata
4. Iris versicolor & I. *'Shirley Queen'*
5. Acorus calamus variegatus
6. Orontium aquaticum
7. Myosotis palustris
8. Mentha aquatica & Mimulus luteus

9. Caltha palustris *'Flore Pleno'*
10. Menyanthes trifoliata
11. Water lily *'James Brydon'*
12. Water lily *'Rose Arey'*
13 & 14. Ceratophyllum demersum
(*an aerating plant*)
Throw Hottonia palustris, *a floating
plant into the water.*

Livestock and aftercare

Much animal life will arrive of its own accord, this may include pond-skaters, whirlygig beetles, frogs, toads and newts. Some of it will clean your pool, so you shouldn't need chemical cleaners. At one stage, tadpoles eat minute plants like algae, that discolour the water, so put some frog-spawn in your pool. Curly ramshorn snails also help in this way. Avoid long pointed water snails, because they eat plant leaves.

Divide up any plants that take up too much space and pull out any blanket weed by hand; it looks like a cloudy patch in the water and the long, hair-like green threads combine into a solid mat to choke other plants and small fish.

Avoid rapidly spreading plants such as *Mimulus guttatus* which is sometimes included by garden centres in 'bargain bundles for beginners'. It can take over your pond.

Use floating pellets to feed the fish so that you know you are only giving them as much as they can eat within a few minutes and there is none left over to rot. The fish won't need feeding at all in cold weather.

If the pool freezes over in winter don't try to crack the ice with a hammer and give the fish concussion: make holes at each end by standing saucepans of hot water on the ice. This will allow gases to escape and keep the water fit for the fish.

Aftercare consists of keeping the pool topped with water, and keeping rubbish and leaves out. Use a small fishing net to clear the surface when necessary in the summer. In autumn when the leaves begin to fall cover the pool by stretching a large net over it - weighed down with stones at the edges.

Maintenance plants

Keeping the water transparent and clean is as essential to water gardening as weeding is to the surrounding garden. Discolouration can be due to too much organic matter in the pond, which encourages algae to spread: chemical fertilizers can also adulterate the water and encourage algae growth.

Certain submerged water plants (the oxygenators) help to eliminate algae; they also provide food for fish and protect them with shade and a hiding place and also provide a nursery where eggs can be laid and safely developed.

You can't have too much life and submerged vegetation in a new pool. Allow 10 plants to each square yard of pond surface. Some of the best plants for keeping the water clean are the elodeas, myriophyllum, *Ceratophyllum demersum* and *Hottonia palustris*.

Anacharis (syn. Elodea) canadensis

Some suggested plant combinations for the pool and surrounds

Spring

Pool margins: Blue, water forget-me-nots with golden marsh marigolds (*Caltha palustris*) and pink-and-white scrambling bogbeans (*Menyanthes trifoliata*).

Bold *Lysichitum americanum*, which has 2-foot yellow flowers alongside double, golden marsh marigolds (*Caltha palustris* 'Plena').

Boggy surrounds: White snowflakes (*Leucojum vernum*) with pussy willows, marsh orchids in grass, and white narcissi.

Gold and yellow trollius with purple and black chequered *Fritillaria meleagris* and blue camassias.

Summer

Red water lillies in the pool (see below) with marginals:

Blue *Pontederia cordata* and pink flowering rushes (*Butomus umbellatus*).

Acorus calamus 'Variegatus' (which looks like a green and white variegated iris before it produces brown poker-like inflorescences).

Blue *Iris laevigata*.

Yellow or white water lilies in the water make striking companions with the yellow water fringe *Hydrocleys nymphoides* too.

In the pool's boggy surrounds try: Pink and white astilbes with blue *Iris sibirica* and some feathery white, bold-leaved rodgersias;

Iris sibirica with pink and red *Primula pulverulenta*, ferns and blue meconopsis;

Hostas and astilbes, which make wonderful combinations;

An arrangement of day lilies with scarlet *Lobelia fulgens* and red and yellow mimulus.

Autumn

With red lilies in the water try blue *Pontederia cordata* with white arrowheads and variegated rushes on the pool margins.

Surrounding the pool you could have red berried actaeas, pink lythrums and yellow ligularias.

Or try blue aconitums with blue *Gentiana asclepiadea* and purple-leaved phormiums.

Winter

Prettiest is scarlet and pink-berried pernettyias with pink and white heathers.

Plants in the pool

Water lilies all over.

In shallow water: (under 1 foot) Yellow 'Pygmaea Helvola'; White 'Pygmaea Alba'; Red 'Ellisiana'; 'Paul Hariot' - pinkish ageing to yellow.

In medium depth water (1½ - 2½ feet): Red 'James Brydon'; Pink 'Rose Arey'; Deep Crimson 'Escarboucle'; White 'Gonnere'; Rosy red 'Gloriosa' Yellow 'Sunrise'.

In deep water (2½ feet): White 'Gladstoniana'; Yellow 'Colonel Welsh'; Pink 'Nymphaea Tuberosa Rosea'.

THE EDIBLE GARDEN

A kitchen garden is not for the lazy, such as myself or those who are short of time. It is more demanding than almost every other garden. In the first place you have to start all over again each year, because you have eaten the previous year's garden. Very few of the plants in it are perennial; asparagus, rhubarb and soft fruit, for example. Moreover, you have to keep a more constant eye on vegetables and fruit than you need on flowers or shrubs, to see that nothing is going to leave you with starvation staring you in the face.

Vegetables

The basic thing to remember is to rotate your crops, that is, not to grow the same kind of crop in the same spot each year. This improves the fertility of the soil and cuts down the risk of disease building up. Divide the vegetable plot into three parts:

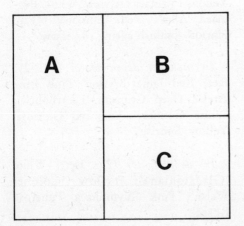

A. Manure it in autumn and plant peas, beans, onions, leeks, lettuces, celery.

B. Lime it in winter and later fertilize it shortly before sowing or planting; plant the cabbage family (including cauliflowers, Brussels sprouts, broccoli) and also spinach.

C. Just fertilize it as above and grow root crops and potatoes.

For the following year everything moves along one: B (lime, fertilizer and cabbages) shifts to the place which was A the year before. C moves over to B and A moves into C. Simple.

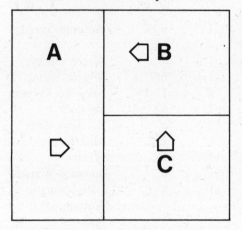

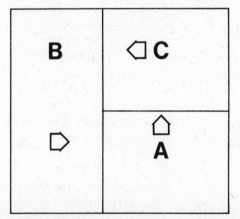

During dry weather in the growing season keep the earth moist by watering well when necessary (see the basic art of watering p.74).

Don't let *pests* eat your food before you can get at it. Every week check for the all-too-obvious signs and spray with vegetable insecticide such as COM-BAT: you can pick your crop the day after spraying it.

If you're going to bother with a genuine vegetable garden I suggest you concentrate either on growing the most expensive vegetables, or on your greatest favourites, so that you can have them fresh and so enjoy them at their best. The prettiest ones (which can be grown in flowerbeds and borders) are globe artichokes; potatoes; rhubarb; perennial broccoli and asparagus (not difficult to grow if you buy the roots). The fewer different items you grow in your first season, the less you have to think about.

*Dig your seed bed on a dry day well before the first frost.

*Dig, tread down and rake your seed bed.

*Before sowing or planting, fertilize soil.

*Don't sow in wet, soggy soil, but in moist soil.

*Buy best quality seeds and plants and don't sow them too deep or too thickly.

*Thin seedlings out fast, firm-in and water gently, then fertilize.

*Don't grow the same sort of crop in the same place year after year.

*Rotate your crops - root or brassica (cabbagey vegetables) *or* the rest.

*Manure well to increase the water-holding capacity of the soil.

*Remember (page 27) too much fertilizer is harmful. Do not apply more fertilizer prior to sowing or planting if soil has already been fertilized.

VEGETABLE SOWING AND PLANTING GUIDE

Name	Sow/Plant (S/P)	Distance Between Rows	and Plants	When to Eat
Artichokes (Jerusalem)	(P) Very early Spring	2½-3'	1'	Winter-Spring
Onion	(S) Early Spring (P) Spring	1'	6"	Autumn-Spring
Leeks	(S) Early Spring	1'	9"	Winter-Spring
Parsnip	(S) Early Spring	1-1½'	6-9"	Winter-Spring
Early Potatoes	(P) Early Spring	2'	12-15"	Summer-Autumn
Broad Beans	(S) Early Spring	2'	6"	Summer
Pea	(S) Early Spring	2-5'	3"	Early Summer
Radish	(S) Early Spring	1'	1-2"	Mid-Spring
Seakale	(P) Early Spring	1½'	1'	Winter
Shallots	(P) Early Spring	1'	6"	Summer-Winter
Spinach	(S) Early Spring	1'	8"	Late Spring-Autumn
Early Carrots	(S) Early Spring	1'	3'	Summer
Summer Lettuce	(P) Spring	1'	9"	Spring-Autumn
Summer Cauliflower	(P) Spring	2'	2'	Summer-Early Autumn
Artichokes (Globe)	(P) Spring	2½-3'	2'	Summer-Early Autumn
Asparagus	(P) Spring	1-1½'	1'	Late Spring-Early Summer
Broccoli (sprouting)	(S) Spring	2'	2'	Early-Late Spring
Summer Cabbage	(S) Spring (P) Spring	2'	2'	Summer
Autumn Cabbage	(S) Spring	2'	2'	Autumn
Winter Cabbage	(S) Spring	2'	2'	Late Autumn-Winter
Main Crop Potatoes	(P) Spring	2½'	15"	Early Autumn-Late Spring
Rhubarb	(P) Spring	3'	3'	Spring-Summer
Onion (sets)	(P) Spring	1'	6"	Late Summer-Spring
Beetroot	(S) Spring	1'	4-6"	Summer
Summer Cauliflower	(S) Spring (P) Spring-Early Summer	2'	2'	Summer-Autumn
Autumn Cauliflower	(S) Spring	2'	2'	Autumn
Winter Cauliflower	(S) Late Spring	2'	2'	Winter-Spring
Tomatoes	(P) Spring-Early Summer	2'	1½'	Late Summer-Early Autumn

Turnips	(S)	Spring - Early Summer	1'	9"	Early Summer - Autumn
Marrows	(S)	Spring	3-4'	3-4'	Summer-Autumn
	(P)	Spring - Early Summer			
Radishes	(S)	Spring - Late Summer	1'	1-2"	Spring-Early Autumn
Main Crop Carrots	(S)	Late Spring	1'	6"	Early Autumn - Late Spring
Celeriac	(P)	Late Spring	1½'	1'	Autumn-Winter
Celery	(P)	Late Spring	1-1¼'	1'	Summer-Winter
French Beans	(S)	Late Spring	2'	9"	Summer
Runner Beans (10" between a double staggered row. 6' between each pair of such rows)	(S)	Very Late Spring	10"	9"	Summer Autumn
	(P)	Late Spring			
Beetroot	(S)	Late Spring	1'	4-6"	Summer-Spring
Brussel Sprouts	(S)	Spring	2½'	2'	Autumn-Spring
	(P)	Late Spring			
Summer Lettuce	(S)	Late Spring-Summer	1'	9"	Late Spring-Early Autumn
Swedes	(S)	Early Summer	1'	9"	Early Autumn - Early Spring
Leeks	(P)	Early Summer	1'	9"	Autumn-Spring
Broccoli (sprouting)	(P)	Early Summer	2'	2'	Winter-Early Spring
Autumn Cabbage	(P)	Early Summer	2'	2'	Autumn
Autumn Cauliflower	(P)	Early Summer	2'	2'	Autumn
Chicory	(S)	Early Summer	1'	8"	Autumn-Winter
Radish	(S)	Early Summer	1'	1-2"	Mid-Late Summer
Winter Cauliflower	(P)	Summer	2'	2"	Winter-Spring
Onion	(S)	Summer	1'	6"	Summer-Autumn
Winter and Red Cabbage	(P)	Midsummer	2'	2'	Winter
Winter/Spinach	(S)	Mid Summer	1'	8"	Mid Autumn-Winter
Winter Spinach	(S)	Late Summer	1'	8"	Late Autumn-Winter
Spring Lettuce	(S)	Late Summer	1'	6"	Spring
	(P)	Autumn			
Spring Cabbage	(S)	Late Summer	1½'	1½'	Spring
	(P)	Very Early Autumn			
Broad Beans	(S)	Late Autumn	2'	6"	Summer

Edible gardens

The best place for a herb garden is near the kitchen. Here is an informal planting of lovage, chervil, sage and hyssop.

Michael Warren

Michael Warren

A kitchen garden is not for the lazy but you can create a pretty garden of flowers and vegetables, choosing vegetables as much for their looks as for taste.

Jerry Harpur

Plants for disguise
You will always need a space for the utilities of the garden. Make a feature of tool sheds or hide a more unsightly compost heap with a screen of climbing plants.

Neil Holmes

Garden furniture

Furniture in a garden has a way of hogging the limelight and becoming the major focal point. Frances Perry in her garden makes a special feature out of a garden seat, wreathing it with petunias and nasturtiums.

Neil Holmes

If you want to leave the furniture in the garden, choose from synthetic resin, aluminium or tubular alloy.

THE MICRO VEGETABLE GARDEN

Even if you have only a bare patch of paving stone outside the back door or on a balcony you can put tubs there and triumphantly watch delicious things grow in them, with practically no effort on your part. Grow them in magic bags. GRO-BAGS contain compost that's already mixed with fertilizer; you just make two or three holes in the top, in which to plant your tiny lettuces, tomatoes or cucumbers. Make no drainage system (that's holes in the bottom, to you) but keep the compost moist and don't overwater it. Added bonus - soilless compost is virtually disease and pest free.

You can grow marrows, courgettes and French beans in tubs, and you can also start runner beans in them and train them up canes. You can grow strawberries in large pots. If you prise up a couple of stone slabs in a path or terrace (an excellent reason, incidentally for not laying permanent floors), you will have two pockets of soil in which you can grow gooseberries and redcurrant cordon; a cordon is not a bush, but a single stem, like a walking stick, planted so that it slopes away from the sun.

If you haven't a back door patch, then provided your kitchen has enough light you can grow a micro vegetable garden in a window box: try garlic, salad onion, French beans, lettuce or mustard and cress (which only takes 10 days to mature, as opposed to asparagus which takes over 3 years). You might also try pretty dwarf tomato plants. Buy little plants in April or May and don't overwater them or they go mouldy. Incidentally, tomato plants also make cheerful *indoor* kitchen displays and are a good idea for offices, instead of those seedy, old '60s rubber plants.

90

If you garden in tubs or window boxes or GRO-BAGS, rather than direct into the earth, fill whatever container you choose with a first-rate compost and remember that plants, like new-born babies, are dependent on you for their food and drink. (Perhaps give them a drink when you have one in the evening.) Feed occasionally with a general liquid fertilizer; with a low nitrogen content. (Pick a rose fertilizer rather than one formulated for pot plants and high in nitrogen).

If your space and time is limited, grow only those plants that will give you the best value. Here they are:

BEANS (FRENCH, BROAD)

Drawback   These, and even runner beans may prove more bother than other vegetables recommended here.

CARROTS (Short rooted varieties, such as Kundulus, Early French Frame, or Suko)

Bonus Points Very pretty, frothy foliage.

Drawback   As more carrots than onions are usually needed in a recipe, you won't get so much value per dish.

GARLIC

Bonus Points A little of it goes a long, long way. A spacesaver. Sometimes difficult to buy in shops.

LETTUCE Choose 'Tom Thumb', a small, sweet, crisp cabbage-shaped lettuce, and 'Little Gem' which looks like a miniature Cos.

Bonus Points Quick growing (should see results in 10 weeks). Grow 4" apart. unbelievably good if cut a few minutes before eating.

MUSTARD AND CRESS

Bonus Points Amazing speed, should see results in 10 days.

MINI CUCUMBERS

Disadvantages An indoor starter. Treat as sweet peppers. When big enough, transfer to 4 inch pots or window box. At this point, provide stakes to 'loop' the growth (up a bamboo one side and down the other) with a crosspiece.

RADISHES. Choose 'Cherry Belle' or 'Saxa'

Bonus Points Quickest crop. Should see results in 6 weeks.

SHALLOTS. A triple purpose vegetable. Slice it, raw, into salad; add to cooking dishes for a delicate onion flavour: use when mature as a pickling onion.

SWEET PEPPERS. Choose Triton (green), Yellow Lantern (yellow), Canape F1 (deep red).

Bonus Points Very pretty, quick growing. Expensive in shops.

Disadvantages Peppers have to be started *indoors*, on a window sill in 4 in. pots; you can put the pots out or transfer them to window boxes in very late spring. They need short bamboo stakes to support them, once they are laden with fruit. A *daily* light misting of the flowers (use a water squirter) helps to 'set' the fruit.

TOMATOES. Choose Minibel.

Bonus Points Fun to watch.

Disadvantages Not much flavour. An indoor start. Treat as sweet peppers. Feed weekly once the flowers appear.

HAPPY HERBS-HOW AND WHEN TO GROW AND EAT THEM

The best place for a herb garden is near the kitchen. It may be in the garden itself or on a small scale - in a window-box or in pots on a window-sill in summer; the pots can be brought inside in winter.

Bay, rosemary, thyme and winter savory are evergreens, so your window-box will always look good and green.

Herbs that are easy to grow but which require regular renewal or division are parsley, chives, tarragon, basil, marjoram and rocket.

It's relatively 'easy to remember' to water a window-box regularly, because all you have to do when clearing breakfast is to open the window, with a saucepanful of water in one hand .... Some herbs, such as chives, will even grow in the kitchen, but others can't stand the smell of cooking before it's their turn, or can't stand the heat. Four or five-inch flower pots are usually big enough. Put broken crocks in the bottom of the pots for drainage.

Grow annuals (1 year only) from seed. Perennials, which go on growing for years if you're lucky are best bought as well-established plants from a nursery or garden centre and stuffed straight into pots of soilless compost, which should be kept *just* moist and never over-watered. Don't use garden soil, it's full of weeds and diseases.

Feed occasionally (try once a week) with a liquid feed. Choose a general fertilizer: don't use a feed that's too high in nitrogen (such as BABYBIO) or you may get long, leggy weak plants.

This is what you plant and you do it in mid-spring, unless otherwise mentioned.

Always keep some cuttings growing in reserve, as replacements or as gifts.

BALM: Hardy perennial.

BASIL: A half-hardy annual, easier to grow inside than out, so plant indoors in early spring and gradually pot up. Sow seeds outdoors in late spring to early summer. Don't buy bush basil, only sweet or lemon.

BAY: Hardy and pretty evergreen shrub. Best bought from a nursery as a pot plant. Grows very large, if not clipped. Best bought as small growing plant.

CHIVES: Flourish in window-boxes, even in town. The leaves can be cut back (half or more) in the early part of the year: they should be cut repeatedly so that new leaves continue to sprout.

DILL: Graceful annual, very easy to grow from seed; in fact the problem is restraining the plants from taking over the window; they tend to grow like triffids. Pinch out the growing tips regularly to keep the plant bushy.

FENNEL: Hardy perennial. Plant outdoors from spring to early summer. Keep trim by pinching back growing shoots.

MINT: Plant from seed or by dividing a friend's plant (page 67) at any time from spring to autumn. Needs good soil and moisture and some shade. Mint can be very invasive and is best grown in a mini-GRO BAG, which keeps it in one place.

PARSLEY: Biennial, which runs to seed in the second year, so use it up and sow it annually. It can take a couple of months to germinate so don't give up hope. "Triple Curled" is best for pot growing, and will probably survive being brought into the kitchen in winter, but doesn't like being indoors.

ROCKET: Why not a rare herb to boast about? Rocket was, reputedly, King Charles II's favourite salad vegetable. An annual. Sow direct, where it is going to grow.

ROSEMARY: Evergreen perennial. Grow from 6 inch cuttings in spring or autumn, bring indoors during winter frosts. Must be kept neat and bushy by pinching back growing shoots. Grows to a very large bush if not clipped.

SAGE: Hardy perennial. Buy dwarf garden sage, which is more compact than the floppy broad-leaved sage. It needs a sunny situation.

WINTER
SAVORY: Small, evergreen shrubby plant. Sow seed in dryish soil.

SWEET
MARJORAM: It is a delicate perennial, so best treat as an annual and grow from seed outdoors in late spring to early summer. Needs sun and warmth.

TARRAGON: Don't buy inferior Russian tarragon, buy perennial French tarragon. Buy rooted cuttings or small growing clumps. Multiply it by division, if you want to keep a constant supply of new plants.

THYME: Small hardy shrub. Grow from cuttings in early summer.

Which herbs to use with what

BALM: Add a few finely chopped leaves to iced tea.
In egg and milk dishes.
In salads and sauces for fish dishes.

BASIL: Add only at the last moment, to cooked dishes, or you won't taste it.
Add to tomato juice, or tomato sauce.
Sprinkle over tomato salad.
Spaghetti sauce.
Spinach or potato soup.
Beef, lamb or veal roasts and stews.
Scrambled egg.

BAY LEAVES: Use the leaf whole.
Add to:
Tomato sauce for pasta.
Poaching fish in milk.
Consomme, chicken and vegetable soups.
Chicken or rabbit casserole.
Beef, lamb or veal stew.

CHIVES: With cold meats: egg and cheese dishes (particularly omelette).
Garnish for chilled soups.
Chop into salads.

DILL: Fish sauces.
To flavour vinegar and pickles.
In green salads.

FENNEL: With fish, veal and pork.
Use leaves for soup.
With cabbage.

MINT: With vinegar as sauce for roast lamb.
With peas or pea soup.
In fruit juices. For mint tea.
With melon.
Chopped into cream cheese.

PARSLEY: As a garnish.
With fish, shellfish and tartare sauce.
Beef, lamb or veal stews.
Chicken or vegetable soups.
Potato salad.
Chop into salads.

ROCKET: Chop into salads.
Try it added to casseroles at the last minute. It has a strong taste, so use little.

ROSEMARY: With roast or stewed lamb or chicken.
With baked fish.
Chicken or tomato soups.
With cauliflower or potatoes.

SAGE: For stuffing (of course) with onion.
With pork, veal, chicken or turkey casseroles.
Sprinkled over fried chicken.
With onions or tomatoes.

SWEET
MARJORAM: Add only at the last minute to cooked dishes, or you won't taste it.
Liver pâté.
Stews and stuffings.

Sprinkled over fried chicken or roast duck.
With baked or grilled fish.
Tomato, potato or vegetable soups.

WINTER
SAVORY: Aromatic, spicy, peppery quality. Use when cooking green beans or for flavouring dressing for a bean salad. Minced savory added to the bread crumb coating on veal is delicious.

TARRAGON: Don't confuse fresh French tarragon with dried tarragon, which is so reminiscent of dried hay.
Wonderful chopped into salad dressing or into wine vinegar or onto roast duck or roast lamb or veal.
Egg dishes.
Potato, tomato or green salad.

THYME: Liver Pâté.
Cottage cheese.
Tomato, mushroom or vegetable soups.
Tomato sauce or juice.
Roast chicken, duck and turkey.
In stews (particularly rabbit stew).
With onions and potatoes.

GARDEN PROBLEMS, PESTS AND WEEDS AND...
how to eliminate them

Unlike human relationships, it's amazing how quickly disinterest turns to passion in the matter of pest control when the beginner-gardener finds her roses being holed and her potatoes showing signs of gangrene.

It's not possible to pass through life without encountering a few pests. In the garden *everyone* - expert and beginner - suffers them, but at least there you can destroy them.

Different plants attract different pests and diseases; some problems are the result of specific weather conditions. For example, slugs like it wet; greenfly like it dry.

There are two kinds of cure, cultural and chemical.

Cultural cures. These are basically preventative and involve preparing the garden thoroughly so that your plants have the very best chance of living a healthy life.

Most plants dislike waterlogged ground; their roots will rot if the soil is poorly cultivated. If the soil has been poorly cultivated over a long period of time, a hard layer of soil - impermeable to water - may form beneath the soil surface. So, dig thoroughly and if you have a heavy, sticky soil work in plenty of well-rotted compost, peat or even a coarse grit. Remember never to mix the subsoil with the precious, fertile topsoil. The compost will improve the texture of the soil so helping the water to drain away and allowing the plant roots to breathe.

Other cultural measures include buying fresh seed and healthy plants, sowing and planting at the right time, taking note of all instructions on seed packets, making sure that you feed your plants properly, and never leaving rubbish or old plants about to attract woodlice and the like.

Chemical cures. Chemicals are safe to use provided you follow the manufacturers' instructions: Read the instructions carefully; always respect the time lapse recommended by manufacturers between sowing and eating; always keep chemicals where children can't get them.

Never keep chemicals in unlabelled bottles (especially not in empty drink bottles). When using chemicals in the garden, protect your hands (rubber gloves) and eyes (sunglasses), *even if the instructions don't mention it.* Never spray on a windy day; don't spray near ponds or during blossom time. Always throw away surplus spray immediately and thoroughly rinse out the sprayer.

There are basically three kinds of chemical cures:
insecticides for insects and other pests;
fungicides for diseases;
herbicides for weeds.

Recently, sensible manufacturers have stopped calling these chemical cures by chemical names, preferring to label them according to the pest or disease they are designed to eradicate. So, for example, if you suspect greenfly you simply choose Fison's GREEN-FLY KILLER, no need to have a degree in chemistry.

During summer, check every week for signs of pests to exterminate or diseases to curb. Diseases or insects can ruin your flowers and destroy your food crops; they can affect leaves, shoots, flowers in bud or in bloom, fruit, vegetables, roots and lawn grass. If you suspect a problem you can almost certainly get a specific cure, so make a visit to your local nursery or garden centre .

ERADICATING WEEDS

There are two sorts of weed: *annual* (such as groundsel, speedwell, shepherd's purse), which seed themselves so make sure you remove them *before* they flower; and *perennial* (such as nettles and docks). Perennials are the real problem and will return again and again unless you root them out and destroy both plant and *all* its roots, preferably by burning.

A weed is a plant that is insensitive to insult. They are often pretty, but because they're so tough they can choke your plants or starve them to death by using all the available space, light and nourishment in the soil. Weeds can also harbour insects and diseases.

What to use. For annuals a hoe is often sufficient.

PROBLEM WEED KILLER (Fisons)	Perennial weeds hate this. It is absorbed through the foliage so apply it when the weeds are in leaf.
SUPERWEEDEX (Murphys)	Designed to clear neglected areas, it works through the soil. But, you won't be able to use the ground for a year afterwards.
TUMBLEWEED (Murphys)	Probably the best weedkiller you can buy, but it takes time to act; read the instructions carefully.
EVERGREEN (Fisons)	All-purpose lawn weedkiller, combined with fertilizer.
WEEDOL (ICI)	For weeds around trees, fruit, shrubs and bulbs, it is ecologically okay because it affects only the green parts of plants, not brown stems or soil. You can plant directly after applying it.

For advice on specific problems, write to the Weed Control Organization, Begbroke Hill Sandy Lane, Yarnton, Oxford. Ask for their leaflet 'Chemical weed control in your garden'.

CURING DISEASE

Disease can become a frustrating and time-consuming problem, with mildew, grey mould and various leaf spots all ruining the appearance of your plants, if not actually killing them. A plant grown in ideal conditions is less likely to suffer disease, but for all sorts of reasons the artificial conditions of town gardens encourage plant sickness. Some plants are more prone to disease than others. For instance, the rose 'Peace' will remain healthy while 'Frensham' will get covered in mildew, to which it isn't resistant. Most antirrhinums and hollyhocks get a fungus called rust, but there are some modern varieties which are rust-proof. Again, some Michaelmas daisies are mildew-proof.

Mildew and blackspot are the commonest problems. A white powdery deposit on leaves is a sign of the first, and black spot is recognizable (not surprisingly) by the appearance of black spots on leaf surfaces. BENLATE is the answer for both of these. Follow instructions for mixing, and spray on at the first sign of disease and again one week later.

Brown, red or orange spots appearing on the underside of leaves signify *rust*. For this either apply DITHANE HEXYL PLUS or pick off the affected leaves.

KILLING PESTS

Unfortunately you will never find plants resistant to greenfly, slugs and snails, all of which flourish in town gardens. There are greenfly sprays, such as ABOL G, that kill only greenfly, not other pests or such insects as ladybirds. You can try to catch snails with a saucerful of diluted beer or protect plants from them by encircling the plants with coarse grit. Slugs hate salt, and Fison's SLUG AND SNAIL KILLER is available in pellet form.

Basically, there are three kinds of pests:

Suckers (such as aphids, greenfly, blackfly). Kill them with Fisons GREENFLY AND BLACKFLY KILLER. But, if you spray this on vegetables or fruit, do not harvest for ten days.

Chewers and biters (such as maggots, weevils, caterpillars). Fisons WHITEFLY AND CATERPILLAR KILLER attacks a broad spectrum of pests – a safe, all-round insecticide for greenhouse and sensitive plants. You could eat your prize marrow or melon the same day as they are sprayed.

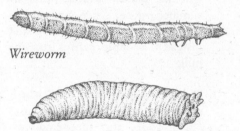

Wireworm

Leatherjacket

Soil pests (such as leatherjackets, wireworms and millepedes) are dealt a deadly blow by Fisons SOIL PEST KILLER. Sprinkle the powder in the area according to the manufacturer's instructions.

FINIS.

TEN MISTAKES ALMOST EVERYONE MAKES

We all make mistakes, and one of our most favourite places for making them is the garden, according to the Gardening Centre at Syon House, Isleworth. These they say, are the 10 most frequent mistakes:

1. We water house plants too frequently but give them too little water so that only the centre of the pot gets wet, while the sides and bottom remain dry. Water plants about once a week on average - depends how hot your house is, and whether it's in winter (less) or summer (more). Then give them a thorough soaking in the sink instead of a couple of drips from the milk jug.

2. We use aerosol insecticides (which are really meant for indoor use) out-of-doors and the wind just blows them away. How the insects laugh!

3. We dash out on the first fine day in spring and scatter the lawn with fertilizer containing weed-killers when it's far too early in the year. This certainly kills the weeds but ruins young grass.

4. We read the instructions on chemical aids *after* using them. It helps to know what you're supposed to do, and since almost every product is different you *can't* just guess or put it right afterwards. So, with whatever you buy, *plough through the instructions before using it.*

5. We plant large trees or what we hope are going to be large trees too close to houses or buildings. Some will actually interfere with house foundations and others, for example the willow are so thirsty that their roots will look for any ways into drains, etc. Keep it at least 40 foot from the house. Keep all large trees out of small gardens.

6. We use unsterilized soil for potting plants or raising seedlings thus exposing baby plants to root rot (Heaven forbid that you should ever learn what this is) and other diseases. Sterilized compost can be bought from your nursery or garden shop.

7. We don't spray plants against pests and disease until the damage has been done. After all, you do *expect* green-fly in June. And then, when we have sprayed, too late, we don't wash out the buckets and sprays that the chemical has been in; this corrodes them.

8. We sow seeds out of doors too early in the year; remember that it's the early bird that gets frostbite.

9. We don't stake herbaceous plants when they are still little; by the time a plant is keeling over, it's too late.

10. We try to grow on limey soil, plants that hate lime - especially rhododendron, camellia, azalea and heathers.

A FEW UNAVOIDABLE PROBLEMS

Even Paradise was never perfect - there was a snake in it. Here is how to slide around a few other garden problems.

Where to put useful, ugly objects

You will always need a space for the utilities of the garden and house - not only compost heaps, but also dustbins, tool sheds, garden-rubbish which needs burning, somewhere to put pot plants while they grow (or recover from sickness), a frame to protect or grow-on plants, a coal bunker or an oil tank.

If you can collect all this kind of thing together in one place, it will save you a lot of to-ing and fro-ing, and give you more space in which to grow plants and enjoy outdoor life. You can hide a compost heap behind screens of climbing plants - honeysuckle, clematis, runner beans or sweet-peas - or use a special container such as the GAROTTA bin, (a chocolate-coloured beast shaped like a Dalek) or the green plastic kind (made of rigid panels which slide up for easy access to finished compost): both have lids.

Animals

Cats, dogs and birds can be catastrophic in town gardens. Flowerbed soil is ideal for a cat's lavatory, as is the seed-bed or window-box. Cover with twigs (prickly if possible) or wire netting, or shake cat-repellent powder about; there is a good, harmless one call SCOOT.

Dogs need exercise, so will gallop round the garden uprooting shrubs and flowers at the slightest excuse; bitches will also leave brown patches on grass. Bitch pee can even kill trees. There's not a lot you can do, except water the brown patches of grass copiously, at once. Alternatively, don't let them into the garden, take them to the nearest park.

Birds

Pigeons, sparrows, starlings and seagulls are also bad news. Don't feed them (except in really cold weather) because it will encourage them: they have all read Parlor's theory. Protect seedlings and young plants with string, cotton, netting or silver kitchen foil hung in strips.

Children

If you have children, you should plan for them. Stop and reconsider what you most want to grow. Children need safe space to run about; soft space is better than hard, so grass is vital, whether it's a lawn or rough grass. There are special mixtures of grass seed which survive constant traffic better than others (see page 69).

Choose really tough plants and shrubs, such as forsythia, syringa, flowering currant and cotoneasters.

Dig out a hole for a sandpit, and if the children are old enough, provide a small pond (with netting over) for endless (silent) fascination by newts, snails, toads and leeches.

Adults

A really good summer party can also leave a lawn looking a wreck. However, grass quickly recovers if you brush it thoroughly the following day having removed all rubbish, such as cigarette ends, matches, food and bottle tops. Water the grass and, in dry weather, give it a boost with a liquid lawn fertilizer.

HOPEFULLY PERENNIAL GARDEN FURNITURE AND ORNAMENTS

At that point in your gardening career when, instead of being bent double, you can look forward to stretching out horizontal, straw hat tilted over forehead and iced drink to hand, you may wish to buy garden furniture.

Garden furniture has a way of hogging the limelight and becoming the major focal point of any garden: it can also be depressing to watch the rain slam down on it in mid-February. So you may decide to invest in collapsible chairs and tables: if so, make sure that they're light to carry and that you have the necessary storage space; you don't want to be assaulted by a multi-lined deckchair every time you reach for the dustpan in the cupboard under the stairs.

If you want to leave the furniture in the garden, choose from synthetic resin, aluminium or tubular alloy: you'll find plenty of decent classic reproductions, as well as Hollywood-style sun-loungers. If you want wood, which always looks good in the garden - choose a weather-resistant hard wood, such as oak, teak or iroka. Avoid one of those fixed-table-come-benches bit of furniture, because you bang and scrape your legs while trying to wriggle into the middle and the whole family will curse it, and it is less adaptable than table and chairs - a false economy. For traditional solid teak outdoor furniture you can't beat the Lister range by GREEN BROS. who supply trad. thirties deckchairs and film-director-style canvas chairs. For free catalogue send sae to Green Bros (Geebro), Summerheath Road, Hailsham, East Sussex BN27 3DT. Tel. 0323 840771. Copies of

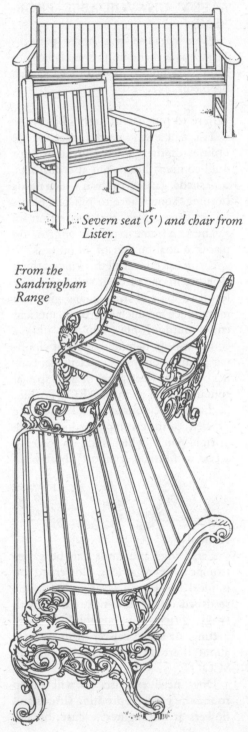

Severn seat (5') and chair from Lister.

From the Sandringham Range

From EMU

The Cumbria Hammock

Patio table &
Rioro chair

Pool bed

The Flip foldaway

Victorian wrought iron furniture can be bought in light aluminium sprayed white. Tables, chairs and benches will not tarnish or rust, (although the wooden slab on the benches may need replacing from time to time). This furniture is for looking pretty and sitting up in, it's not for lounging on, in a bikini. Most of the designs are bastard, tarted-up copies but HALLS JARDINE do a good range called The Sandringham. Write for free catalogue including sae, to Rosemount Tower, Wallington Square, Wallington, Surrey SM6 8RR. Tel. 01 669 8265

If you want garden furniture that is unlikely to rot, fade or rust or warp fast, that is light to carry, folds up easily, takes up very little storage space, is easy to clean by wiping with a damp sponge and can be left outside in rain or sunlight - look at the EMU Gardentime Range, or send sae for free catalogue to The Faversham group, Groveney Road, Faversham, Kent ME13 8UN. Tel. Faversham (079 582) 5511.

Colour and fabric

The best garden furniture colours are white (always for the frame), navy blue and dark green. These blend into the garden colours and fade pleasantly without looking seedy. Plain colour looks better than any pattern: brighter blue is acceptable, a brighter green adds a nasty municipal park touch; any other colour looks as if you're valiantly, but in vain, trying to emulate the Costa Brava in totally alien surroundings. In particular, avoid flowered garden furniture because the manufacturers don't score tops in aesthetics so the flower patterns are always very crude and shown up by the real thing.

Garden ornaments

You'll have no trouble finding gnomes for your garden (or even the up-market equivalent, which is life-size fibreglass deer) but if you want garden ornaments, classic furniture or sculpture, ranging from a few pounds to a more expensive life-sized venus, write to Garden Crafts, 158 New Fulham Road, London SW6. Tel. 01-736 1615.

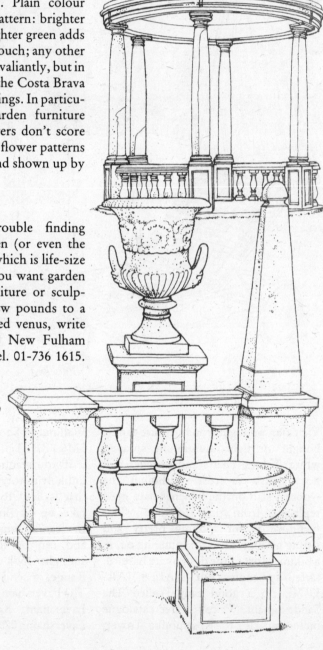

Plenty of simple modern planters, urns and pots in lightweight fibreglass painted black, white or nasty green are available from garden centres but if you want more beautiful (and naturally expensive) garden pots, bird baths, sundials, a wall fountain mask of a satyr, classic stone pond edgings or Elizabethan or Georgian balustrading - then write (sending sae) to Knight Terrace Pots, West Orchard, Shaftesbury, Dorset SP7 0LJ. Tel. Sturminster Newton (0258) 72685.

For really deluxe, stately-home garden statuary in reconstructed limestone that looks a bit like natural Portland stone, write for the sumptuous Haddonstone brochure, from which you can choose paving stones similar to weathered York Stone, balustrading, full-size Corinthian columns, front-door porticos, colonades, fountains, pools, statuary, urns and even your own little Tuscan temple.

Haddonstone also do a lot of restoration carving, with clients ranging from The Church of England to the Duke of Rutland at Belvoir Castle. Write (sending *large* sae) to Haddonstone Ltd., The Forge House, Church Lane, East Haddon, Northampton, NN6 8DB. Tel. East Haddon (060 125) 365.

THE BASIC GARDENER'S CALENDAR

Do not be daunted. This list is to help you to *choose* your own yearly gardening schedule: the beginner's list should be as short as possible:

As weather conditions vary so much between the north and south of the country, this has to be a general guide. Spring and summer usually arrive three or four weeks later in the north and Scotland, while winter comes in earlier - and lasts longer.

Basically, in *winter* you plant indoors in pots, and outdoors, weather permitting, you dig the garden, plant trees and shrubs. In *spring* you add plant-foods, sow seeds, plant seedlings. In *summer* you water and weed and watch. In *autumn* you tidy up, and plant bulbs. And to enlarge on that...

Late winter

Plan gardening year in front of fire. Decide on bulbs (indoor and out), grass (hopefully), vegetable patch (if you don't mind digging) and herbs in kitchen window-box (to disguise mediocre food). Remember not to plant anything that will be at its best when *you* are on holiday. Put in your seed order if not already done (and post it!)

Other Jobs: Apply a potash dressing to fruit trees, bushes and strawberries.
Dig. Dig. Dig.
Manure soil for sowing seeds in spring, (if not done before Christmas).
Stake unstable shrubs and trim.

End of winter/early spring

Dig. Dig. Dig.
Start a seed box or boxes in a warm kitchen, or by a propagator, which is a seed incubator. Fill propagator with JOHN INNES seed compost or Fisons PLANT GROW.

Sow: cauliflower, sprouts, cabbage, and leek seeds. Always sow greens first in a seed bed or box and then transplant them to give them plenty of room to grow.
Sow tomatoes in heated greenhouse or propagator.

Other Jobs: Roses can be pruned in mild areas.
Divide established plants.
Get rid of any wormcasts on lawn by brushing lightly with witch's broom (besom).

Early spring/mid-spring
Dig. Dig. Dig.

Plant: Mint, sage and thyme. Early potatoes. Rhubarb. seakale, leeks, shallots and onion sets (which are onions already partly grown), gladioli (towards the end of month).
Plant and transplant shrubs and trees if not done in previous autumn.

Sow: Many vegetable seeds can be sown outdoors from now on: start with broad beans, leeks, peas, parsnips, carrots, lettuce, onions, radishes, spinach.
Sow celery in boxes in a heated frame. Hardy annuals outside.
New lawns can be sown. Established lawns can enjoy a first mowing, if you must.

Other Jobs: Fork over previously dug soil.
Finish pruning roses.
When soil has had a chance to warm up, mulch fruit trees and bushes to keep weeds away.
Divide and replant established plants.
Rake lawns, then mow (but make sure the blades are set to a high point). If lawn is soggy drain by spiking with a fork and pushing sandy compost into spike holes.
You may find lots of moss in your lawn. Apply moss-killer: when moss has browned, rake out with a springbok (which is a type of rake, not necessarily a rugby player) then spike and re-seed bald patches.
Finish hoeing and digging in borders, although you can't do this if you have lots of bulbs for spring display. If you see shoots of hostas and delphiniums coming up, sprinkle ash or slug pellets around base, otherwise they may disappear!

Mid-spring
Weed, weed, weed, to prevent weeds seeding.

Plant: Asparagus, Globe artichokes, summer cabbages, summer cauliflowers, Sweet peas and gladioli. Evergreen trees and shrubs.

Sow: Sow more seeds out of doors, including peas, beetroot. Sow cucumbers, marrows and melons (in greenhouse or propagator).
Finish sowing of hardy annuals.
Grass seed.
Plant main crop potatoes.

Other Jobs: Remove dead heads from daffodils and other early-flowering bulbs.
Stake any floppy perennials.
Mulch roses. Spray any caterpillar-bound fruit trees after they've finished blossoming.
Mow lawn with medium-height blade. Fertilize.

Late spring
.....can be a busy time.

Plant: Brussels sprouts, celery, and celeriac. Cucumber and melons in greenhouse.
Outdoor flowering chrysanthemums.

Sow: Runner beans, building a cane bean frame for them to climb, or choose dwarf French beans, (which need no support). French and haricot beans, carrots (shorthorn), marrows, peas, turnips, winter cabbage and winter cauliflower in a cosy little corner of the garden, for transplanting later.
Sweet William, Canterbury Bells, wallflowers, foxgloves, Iceland poppies and aquilegias.

Other Jobs: Plant out the seedling cauliflowers, Brussels sprouts, cabbage and leeks you have raised in boxes or beds. If you don't want the trouble of raising them yourself, buy the young plants.
Prune quick growing evergreen hedges and early-flowering shrubs.
Spray roses against diseases and pests, then apply fertilizer. I have a friend who underplants her yellow and cream rosebeds with buttercups, both colourful and unusual.
Reduce space between raspberry canes to 6 inches when tied in.
Weed borders and hoe between your crops. Hoe every day, if possible, because it can cut out nearly all weeding for the next few months.
You've got to start mowing the lawn once a week from now until end sum-

mer. Apply Fison's EVERGREEN 80 to lawn; it feeds and weeds all in one go.

Deal ruthlessly with slugs and snails as they do enormous damage to young plants.

Early summer
A very busy time, especially if you want lots of colourful annuals. Real growing things (peas and beans) start to appear. Intense excitement.
Continue hoeing with added impetus.

Plant: Outdoor tomatoes, leeks, ridge cucumbers and marrows.
Summer bedding plants.

Sow: Last chance to sow peas and runner beans for second crop in the autumn. Sow lettuce, chicory, radishes, turnips and swedes.

Other Jobs: Keep all pests and diseases under control.
Thin crops and hardy annuals if necessary.
Remove side shoots from sweet peas, and suckers from roses.

Put netting over strawberries.
Stop cutting asparagus mid period.
Start thinning out apples, pears, gooseberries and plums.
Stake tall floppy annuals.
Weed between crops and mulch if necessary.

Summer

Plant: All winter greens from seedbed. Strawberry runners if they are strong enough.

Sow: Last chance to sow French beans, winter parsley, spinach, lettuce and radish seed.

Other Jobs: Earth up maincrop potatoes. ('Earth up' means drawing soil with a hoe, up and around the potato stems).
Feed greenhouse tomatoes, also outdoor tomatoes, when first truss has set, or top-dress.
Spray and feed roses.
Mow lawn at least once a week and water if dry.

Prune redcurrants and cordon or espalier apples and pears. Bush forms pruned in winter.
Cut off dead flower heads.
Clip deciduous hedges.

Late summer

Plant: Snowdrops, crocuses, grape hyacinths, scilla, aconites and hardy cyclamen.

Sow: Spring cabbages, onions and winter spinach in outside seedbed for next spring and early summer.

Other Jobs: Water plants regularly - very important.
Remove dead flower heads.
Stake or restake plants if necessary.
Prune raspberries, loganberries and blackcurrants.
Carry on mowing lawn regularly, raising height of cut if lawn is suffering from drought. Apply weedkiller provided no drought.

Take half-ripe cuttings of shrubs you wish to increase or pass on to friends.

Early autumn

Plant: Spring cabbage.
Evergreen trees, shrubs and hedges.
Dutch, English and Spanish varieties of iris. Replant daffodils and narcissi. Plant indoor bulbs.

Sow: Grass seed. A good month for seeding lawns or re-seeding and renovating old lawns.

Other Jobs: Clip hedges. Cut away damaged or diseased branches of cherry and plum trees.
Stake tall asparagus and dahlias.
Take geranium, fuchsia and heliotrope cuttings.
Earth up and feed remaining leeks and celery.
Lift potatoes when haulm (that's what the green part is called when it withers) is decayed. Allow the potatoes to dry off for a few hours and store in the dark (or they go green and become poisonous).

Mid-autumn

Plant: All bulbs (except tulips) should be planted by now.

Plant roses (towards the end of the month).
Best time for planting deciduous shrubs, trees and fruit trees while soil is still warm.

Sow: Nothing.

Other Jobs: General tidying-up period.
Do not remove dead heads of hydrangeas; they form valuable protection for next year's buds.
Remove annuals and remove finished crops.
Prune rambling roses. Cut flowered shoots right down and tie in new growth.
Lift and store root crops, except parsnips, which you dig up as you need them.
Lift and store dahlia tubers and outdoor chrysanthemums, at first sign of frost.
Earth up celery and leeks.
Stop mowing lawn. This is the time to lay turves for new lawn.

Late autumn

Plant: Trees, hedges, shrubs and roses. Tulips.

Sow: Broad beans.

Other Jobs: Tidy up generally.
Clear finished crops (use for compost heap).

Lift and store root crops.
Lift rhubarb roots for early forcing. Remove dead leaves from Brussels sprouts.
Sweep up and store leaves and remove any covering plants.
Divide perennials. Weed. Send off for seed catalogues.
If you have rose beds, clear all weeds by hoeing, then water the entire bed with disinfectant solution (JEYES FLUID) and, to your immense surprise, you will discover that it almost sterilises the soil, which remains free of weeds.
Prune fruit trees.

Winter

Plant: Chicory and rhubarb for forcing. Roses (if mild) and fruit trees.

Sow: Nothing

Other Jobs: Continue pruning fruit trees.
Order seeds and perennial plants from catalogues.
Start digging and manuring empty ground to start all over again.
Then back to the fire with the latest seed catalogues.

ADDRESS BOOK FOR GARDENERS

Nothing is more luxurious than toasting your toes in front of a winter fire and leafing through the mouth-watering seed catalogues: in fact, one and a half million British gardeners shop this way and some of them solve their present problems by buying gift vouchers for their friends. A pound still goes a long way in a seed catalogue!

Many catalogues (published around November - write before they run out) are sent to you *free* - sometimes over 100 pages of temptingly inexpensive flowers, herbs and vegetables: in fact some people send off for ALL of them. If not free, the charge is minor.

THOMPSON AND MORGAN have a most unusual vegetable selection, including saffron-yellow vegetable spaghetti, kohl rabi and burpless cucumbers. They're bean freaks, offering not only mung, oriental adzuki and soya bean sprouts, but showing how to grow them in a jam jar. They also include a section on trout and carp farming equipment, using a small ornamental pond in your garden, as did medieval monks. Their herbal remedies give instructions for growing the herbs, how to prepare and use them (cat nip for indigestion, horehound for warding off colds and so on).
(Thompson & Morgan, London Road, Ipswich, Suffolk IP2 0BA.
Tel. Ipswich (0473) 218821).

SUTTONS are famous for their beautifully produced catalogue, which also contains simple gardening articles and a few vegetarian recipes. One of their specialities is different grass seeds and I can recommend their 'Green Glade' seed for city gardens such as mine, which rarely see the sun.
(Sutton Seeds Ltd., Hele Road, Torquay, Devon TQ2 7QJ.
Tel. Torquay (0803) 62011).

DOBIES specialize in summer-flowering bulbs and gardening equipment such as soil-test kits, compost bins, weasels for seed bed preparation and green slime remover. They also have a club with special money saving offers, *a free advisory service, free samples of new varieties* and *free or reduced entrance fees to certain stately homes and gardens.*
(Samuel Dobie & Sons Ltd., Upper Dee Mills, Llangollen, Clwyd LL20 8SD.
Tel. Llangollen (0978) 860119).

THOMAS BUTCHER specialize in sub-tropical plants for the greenhouse.
(Thomas Butcher Ltd., 60 Wickham Road, Shirley, Croydon, Surrey CR9 8AG Tel. 01 654 3720)

I like MARSHALL'S 'Garden' collection of 21 assorted vegetables for the small garden, and their 'Wisbech' collection is planned to provide a succession of 31 vegetables over the whole year.

(S.E. Marshall & Co. Ltd., Regal Road, Weasenham Lane, Wisbech, Cambs. PE13 2RF. Tel. Wisbech (0945) 3407). All orders are sent *post free*, unless very large.

The advantage of *General Nurseries* is that you're only dealing with one firm and filling in one form. They can supply almost anything from herbaceous plants to water plants and ferns, but perhaps trees, shrubs, climbers, conifers and hedging plants are the most useful to have sent mail order. There are many good general nurseries and specialists, among them:
Hillier Nurseries (Winchester) Ltd., Winchester, Hants SO22 5DN. Tel. Winchester (0962) 69245.
Notcutts Nursery Ltd., Woodbridge, Suffolk. Tel. Woodbridge (03943) 3344)
Scotts Nurseries, Merriott Ltd., Merriott, Somerset. Tel. Crewkerne (04607) 2306.

Grass Mixtures: Shade grass for gardens such as mine which get hardly any sun (try SUTTONS 'Green Glade' mixture). For a lawn that's going to withstand rough, tough use if you have children or pets, try 'Summer Play', or for a beautiful smooth lawn - the sort that bowling greens are made of, smooth yet springy - try 'Summer Day', which is quick to show and slow to grow (so needs less mowing). These seeds are available from SUTTONS SEEDS, Hele Road, Torquay TQ2 7QJ. (Tel. Torquay (0803) 62011).

Small bulb specialists: One of the most heartwarming treats of late winter, when it's still cold and shivery, is the sight of snowdrops and crocuses bravely peering through. Generally they're in other people's gardens and, when you see them, you think "I *wish* I'd done that".
Broadleigh Gardens, Barr House, Bishops Hull, Taunton, Somerset. Tel. Taunton (0823) 86231. Spring list and autumn catalogue.

General bulb specialists: For bigger bulbs, such as lilies, gladioli, begonias and peonies:
P. De Jager & Sons, The Nurseries, Marden, Kent. Tel. Maidstone (0622) 831235. Free catalogue.
Kelway Nurseries, Langport, Somerset. Tel. Langport (0458) 250521 Catalogue - send 10p for postage.
Walter Blom Ltd., Coombelands Nurseries, Leavesden, Watford, Herts. Tel. Garston (092 73) 72071. Free catalogue.

Water plant specialists: When you consider that Britain is so·water-logged most of the year, it's surprising that there aren't more water gardens, particularly in small town backyards.
Jackamoor's Hardy Plant Farm, Theobalds Park Road, Enfield, Middlesex.
Tel. 01 363 4278. Free catalogue.

113

Geranium specialists: Geraniums (pelargoniums) are cheerful, good-tempered indoor plants - every kitchen should have one. They make docile window-box decoration and, wherever they are, they smell like the most expensive soap.

Clifton Geranium Nurseries, Cherry Orchard Road, Whyke, Chichester, Sussex.
Tel. Chichester (0243) 82010. Send 15p for catalogue.

Herb specialists: If you grow your own herbs in a kitchen window-box, flower pot or a patch outside the back door, you will notice the great improvement they make to your food. Use tarragon to disguise that fishy taste in modern chickens (it's not your imagination, they're fed on cheap fishmeal); grow fresh mint for lamb, (once started, the problem is to *stop* it); and persevere with the parsley. (See page 95 'Which Herbs to Use with What').

Grove Farm Nurseries, Brookwood, Nr. Woking, Surrey. Tel. Brookwood (048 67) 2039.
Tumblers Bottom Herb Farm, Kilmersdon, Radstock, Somerset. Tel. Radstock (076 13) 3452. Catalogue 20p.

Rose specialists: You're either a rose person or you're not. You either think they're the most trouble or the least trouble, but undoubtedly one of the advantages of roses is that, with careful choosing, you can have roses, roses all the way, from early summer to Christmas.

John Mattock Ltd., Nuncham Courtenay, Oxford. Tel. Nuncham Courtenay (086 738) 265. Catalogue - send 10p for postage.

Herbaceous plant specialists: For stocking your borders and filling the blanks between flowers, trees and grass.
Bressingham Gardens, Diss, Norfolk. Tel. Bressingham (037 988) 464. Send stamped addressed envelope for catalogue.

Garden equipment: (See also pp. 102-105, *Garden Furniture*) Abermule Nurseries, Abermule, Montgomeryshire. Tel. Abermule (068 686) 203. Cast iron garden furniture.
Fisons Horticultural Division, Paper Mill Lane, Bramford, Ipswich, Suffolk IP8 4BZ. Tel. Ipswich (0473) 830492. Fertilizers, peat, potting composts etc. will supply leaflets.
Haddonstone, The Forge House, Church Lane, East Haddon, Northants. Tel. East Haddon (060 125) 365. Reproduction stone urns. Catalogue.
Pan Britannica Industries, Waltham Cross, Herts. Tel. Waltham Cross (97) 23691. Chemicals, potting mixtures. Will supply leaflets.

For further information about suppliers and a list of mail-order suppliers, each of whom accept and sell National Garden Gift Tokens, write to:
The Horticultural Trades Association, 18 Westcote Road, Reading, Berkshire. Tel Reading (0734) 581371.

2

THE GREAT INDOORS

The indoor plant guide

If you haven't got much (or any) garden, you might try indoor gardening. It's harder for the plants but easier for you, and if you live in a concrete jungle you can at least be reminded of the great outdoors beyond by delicate green ferns, green leaves and a few friendly flowers.

House plants cause most of us as much trouble as children, they need endless fussing over, you can't leave them alone for long, and they keel over with mysterious diseases. But if you remember that, like caged birds, most of them have been wrenched from a tropical climate and made to grow under artificial conditions, it's not surprising that they have trouble staying alive.

How can you be a happy house plant owner? The answer is simple; pick the kind of plants that can and will stand your climate - particularly if it's the average British indoor climate - and you're halfway there. The next thing to consider is the basic shape. I trained as a sculptor, so perhaps I'm overfussy about these things but I think in terms of a basic sculptural shape for a certain place in a room, I look first for overall form in a plant, I can't stand stragglers or scraggy plants. I like a thick, strong line to the thing.

Thirdly, you look at the leaves to check that they're like a dog's nose - slightly glistening and slightly damp with no moth-eaten edges (except for the Swiss Cheese Plant) and then you look at the bottom to check that the roots aren't coming out.

Best survivors

Here's my choice of Good Tempered Plants, that will thrive in *almost* all likely conditions, and also look after themselves reasonably well.

AECHMEA: A jungle-born bromeliad which has its own built-in vase to collect water. It has striking fleshy foliage, red rosettes and needs plenty of light.

ASPIDISTRA: A hardy plant - also known as the cast-iron plant - with long dark green leaves and occasional purpleish flowers. The Victorians knew what they were doing when they featured this in the draughty drawing room. It thrives in gloom, needs little light and not much water. Wonderful for bachelors.

BEGONIA SEMPERFLORENS: A low-growing plant with dozens of tiny flowers in pinks, purples, reds and whites - the window box flower. It also goes well in hanging baskets and will flower from spring to autumn.

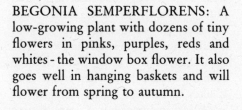

CHLOROPHYTUM COMOSUM 'VARIEGATUM': The Spider Plant, with its green and white striped leaves and plantlets on the tip of the flowers. If it is to keep its two-tone colour it should be kept moist and in. medium light. Basically good-tempered.

117

COLEUS: Flame Nettle, a foliage plant with red, green, yellow, white and bronze centres to its leaves. This is one you can even grow outdoors in summer, or leave in the back garden for a holiday when you go away. It needs sun to keep its colour (though not direct sunlight).

DIEFFENBACHIA: An elegant plant with large leaves sometimes known as Dumb Cane, because with some varieties, if you get the sap in your mouth your tongue swells and you can't speak (so keep it away from children even if there are times when you wish...) It likes to be kept warm, draught-free and moist in summer in a peaty potting mixture.

DRACAENA FRAGRANS: Another one for foliage, with wide green leaves. This African Plant is like a tropical plant in miniature. Looks marvellous display-ed by itself against a plain wall. Needs semi-shade and humid atmosphere.

FATSIA JAPONICA: The false Castor Oil Plant, with large dark shiny leaves, that will stand almost any extreme of temperature. Its leathery leaves look a bit like those of the horse chestnut tree.

FERNS: Do not give much trouble for their graceful beauty, as many restaurants can testify. Most ferns grow well in cool to warm rooms, providing they are kept away from draughts, have good light, humidity and moisture at their roots. High humidity is helped if you stand the pot in a bigger pot or container and pack moist peat around it. Don't stand a fern or any indoor plant in water and don't allow it to dry.

FICUS ELASTICA DECORA: That old friend the Rubber Plant from Asia, with large dark oval leaves. An 'architectural' plant. It needs a winter temperature of minimum 55°F (13°C) to do well.

Window boxes
Unplanted, a window box can block up to 15% of the light; sprawling waterfalls of greenery and flowers that spill over the sill are best if light inside the room is important. See p.134.

Jerry Harpur

Indoor plants and light
Avoid strong direct sunlight for everything except cacti, succulents and geraniums. See p.128.

Jerry Harpur

Outdoor tub plantings and indoor pot plants create a natural link between garden and home.

Neil Holmes

Leslie Johns

An indoor display of irises, crocuses, snowdrops, primroses and azalea reflects the springtime garden scene outside (see below).

Michael Warren

Neil Holmes

An ornament backed by interestingly textured greenery and highlighted by colourful flowers beneath can make a very attractive view from inside and out, even in a small garden.

HEDERA: Another name for the large Ivy family, which comes in some pretty variegated forms. The ivies are particularly good for dark corners and, outdoors, for town window boxes in ill-lit corners, and won't outgrow you at an alarming rate. (I've seen a tiny city garden completely covered in ivy and it looked great). They need a moist, cool temperature.

HOWEA: This is the big 6-footer, like they have at the Ritz. Naturally, not cheap, but you certainly get your money's worth: I once kept one for 4 years in my sitting room. It crashed to the ground and died when I was in hospital for 8 weeks and there was nobody to water it; thinking in crass, financial terms, over 208 weeks, I certainly got good value, and my sitting room has never since felt so luxurious. It's the most easy-going of all the plant family, and is often called the Kentia Palm. It can cope with shade quite happily and only needs generous watering in summer.

Rooms that aren't the size of the Ritz could get the lovely parlour palm NEANTHEBELLA.

IMPATIENS WALLERANA: Busy Lizzie, with tiny leaves, almost constantly bears small flowers in red, pink and white. A favourite of mine, probably because it's the easiest plant to raise from cuttings and to grow. Popular for office window sills.

122

MARANTA: Particularly a variety called the Prayer Plant, because its large, dark-splodged leaves fold together in prayer in the dark. Another easy-going plant, it appreciates having its pot stood on damp pebbles; needs full light.

MONSTERA DELICIOSA: Also called the Swiss Cheese Plant. The large leaves have holes and slits in them. Though formless, in my opinion, it's a big plant that can make a good backdrop for other specimens. Likes a bright position away from direct sunlight with moderate humidity.

PELARGONIUM: Usually called a geranium - just about the happiest house plant of all. Take your pick from many popular varieties, with plain leaves or variegated ones, flowers in red, pink, mauves or white. Provided that you don't over-water them, pelargoniums are surprisingly difficult to kill. If the plant looks dead, just water it gently and leave it. It often resurrects itself quite quickly. Can give a show of flowers all year round. Nip off the growing tips to keep the plant bushy.

PEPEROMIAS: Compact, thickly leaved little house plants that like plenty of light but not direct sunlight. Let roots dry out slightly between each watering. When it gets old and untidy you can raise new plants by putting individual leaves erect in a peat and sand mixture. Wish it was as easy as that for us.

PHILODENDRON SCANDENS: The Sweetheart Vine, with heart-shaped leaves. Basically a climber, but if you cut it back it will form a bushy plant. Although it is happiest in the warmth this is an easily-grown stayer that can stand punishment.

PILEA CADIEREI: The best known version is the Aluminium Plant, with long-stalked, silver-streaked leaves. It is a fast-growing house plant that will quickly help to fill out a trough or mixed display. It needs light, but keep out of direct sunlight.

RHOICISSUS RHOMBOIDEA:
Grape Ivy, with large glossy dark leaves.
Tough as old boots, this plant wll grow
almost anywhere - hot or cold places,
moist or dry. It prefers some warmth in
winter and should be kept slightly
moist. A good plant for mixed containers.

SANSEVIERIA: One of which is
Mother-In-Law's Tongue, which has
tall, stiff mottled leaves, some with a
yellow edge to them (quite). Either you
like Sansevieria or you don't. It's just
about the toughest plant of all, blissfully
neglectable. It needs good light,
medium temperature and very little
water.

TRADESCANTIA FLUMINENSIS:
Speedy Jenny is the secretary's favourite
companion, since it will even grow in a
jar of water. It has small silver-streaked
leaves with fleshy trailing stems. It's a
Houdini of a plant, a marvellous choice
for children to start on since you can
almost watch it growing.

Pick any selection of these Top Good
Tempered Plants and you'll soon have a
green-filled interior.

125

PRETTY PARTICULAR PLANTS

AFRICAN VIOLETS: Really prefer Africa and need lots of light and a humid atmosphere in order to continue flowering. They like a temperature of 70°F (21°C) on a north window with plenty of light but no direct sunlight. Try not to get water on the leaves.

AZALEAS: Are the trickiest indoor plant. They like full light. They strongly object to a dry atmosphere. They like to be kept moist, not wet and not over 50°F (10°C) indoors. One way to kill them quickly is to water with cold, hard tap water. Use room-temperature rainwater or distilled water (from chemist or garage) or collect the water when you defrost your fridge. Or give them away quickly to someone who has positively nothing to do.

CINERARIA: Will go on flowering only if it is cool, not more than 60°F (16°C) by day and a little cooler at night.

CYCLAMEN: Difficult. Keep in an even temperature of 55°F (13°C). They like a slightly humid atmosphere. In this case, water the plant from a saucer. (Not like granny drinking tea, I mean *stand* it in a saucer of water). Don't water when conditions are cold, on winter mornings.

ERICA: Those heathers from South Africa. Keep moist. They hate hard water so use distilled water. You can kill them by allowing them to dry out, which they quickly do in the small pot in which they often come as cheap gifts.

POINSETTIAS: Almost more Christmassy than holly, these days, this vulgar plant needs a temperature between 59°F (15°C) and 65°F (18°C). Water sparingly, feed regularly in summer. But why bother at all?

MORAL: If giving indoor plants, give chrysanthemums, which are almost impossible to kill except by *total* neglect. Just water them regularly in order to keep the earth moist. How regularly is regularly? It depends on the heat of your house. Give the soil water when they *start* to look dry. If they look dry, then you should have watered them the previous day.

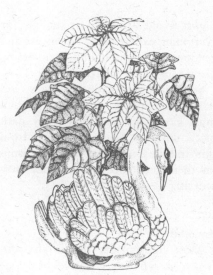

Basic indoor plant care

A plant can have as tough a time surviving indoors as you would outdoors, so try and adjust your natural habitat to it, and in Britain don't get plants that want a dry, hot summer. Like you, a plant needs light, air, moisture, food and to be cleaned occasionally. It also needs a suitable bed. And like you, it catches a chill in a draught.

Situation: The secret of keeping an indoor plant alive is to find the best place for it, then leave it there.

Never move plants from one temperature extreme to another.

Humidity: Most indoor plants need humidity (moisture in the atmosphere, distinctly absent from centrally heated rooms), so stand the pot on pebbles, which are standing in a little water in a saucer or bowl: or grow several plants together in a trough surrounded by damp peat.

Light: Avoid strong direct sunlight for everything except cacti, succulents and geraniums. Bright light for flowering plants, shade for foliage.

Some plants - notably the ivies - will stand comparative gloom, but if you must have a display in a really dark place, dose the plants with light from time to time by training a reading lamp on them (not too near or they may scorch).

Air: Constant temperature: no draughts.

Most houseplants dislike dry air, which is why they thrive better in bathrooms, kitchens or underprivileged homes without any central heating.

Two of the most popular plants that like dry air - and therefore centrally heated rooms - are cacti and geraniums.

Suitable soil: A good potting mixture (get one from a garden centre or where you got the plant) is a blend of peat, plant food and bits of rock to aerate the mixture, so even if you overwater, the roots don't get waterlogged. Potting mixture can also be used for root cuttings and sowing seed.

Plant food: Plants started in a commercial potting mixture generally need feeding after 2 months of active growth. Obviously you don't want stinking manure in your living room. One capful of FISONS LONG-LASTING FEED GRANULES will keep your plant going for up to 4 months. (Why don't Fisons produce one for children?) I also like BABY BIO Liquid Fertilizer, but which feed you choose for your plants is a matter of personal preference, trial and error.

Feed plants only when they are *actively* growing. Always follow the instructions on the label, giving less rather than more. Frequency of feeding depends on the plant and its state: feeding on demand is the rule, but be careful because overfeeding can damage roots and even kill.

Clean: plant leaves when they get dusty. I use one of those French maid feather dusters on a stick, but you can use a soft paint brush or get a sort of plant-kleenex called LEAFSHINE WIPES (Fisons make it).

Occasionally spray indoor plants with a fine mist of soft water; get the plastic bottle with a squirter lever from your local garden centre.

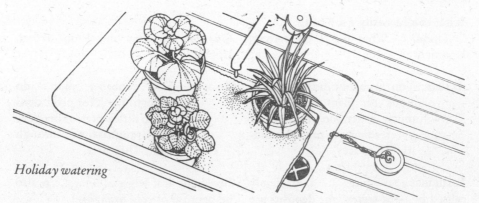

Holiday watering

Watering: (See the basic principles of watering, p 75).

More plants are killed by overwatering than for any other single reason. A plant that has dried out can often be revived, one that has drowned can't. Never overwater - the surface of the soil should be the consistency of a wrung-out flannel. Don't completely dry out before rewatering or you will have damaged the root forever. The art is catching the plant just *before* it looks as if it needs watering. If you are hopeless in gauging when plants need watering, buy a water-meter, which shows you the state of the soil.

When watering, do so thoroughly, so that the water reaches all parts of the pot, which must have a drainage hole in the bottom. Never leave a pot standing in water or the roots will rot.

African Violets, cyclamen, miniature orange and lemon trees should be watered from below.

If the soil fails to absorb water, stand the pot in a bucket of water so that the water is on the same level as the potting mixture. Allow to soak until the soil surface looks wet, then drain.

When you go away on holiday, mock-up an automatic watering system - the most foolproof way to do this is to buy a length of ICI's capillary matting, from a garden centre: put it in the bottom of a sink or bath with the drain clear and a lightly dripping tap, and stand the plants on that.

Repotting: When a plant has grown too large for its pot and its roots begin to show through the base, repot into a slightly larger pot. Before repotting, soak new clay pots in water for several hours or the absorbent clay will draw water out of the soil, and scrub out old pots.

Water the plant the day before, so it's moist but not soggy, then turn it upside down onto your left hand; gently knock the rim of the pot against a table edge and pull it off with your right hand. Be careful of the root: they're the blood vessels, as it were, so don't think a few strands less won't matter. How would *you* feel?

Put an inch or two of potting compost in the bottom of the pot and stand the plant centrally in it. Fill in with more potting compost to ½ inch below rim of pot. Firm down with fingertips, water slowly and leave in the shade for a week.

Never move a plant directly from a small pot into a huge pot. A plant in a 4-inch pot must be transferred to a 7-inch pot before ending up in a 12 inch pot.

What might easily go wrong

Question 1: What did I do wrong, Doctor?

Answer: You probably did too much. Look for plant signs of too much water/too much heat/overfeeding/too much humidity. They are:

Earth that goes white.............probably caused by *hard water lime* deposit: use distilled water

Yellowing leaves which drop off....indicate *overwatering*

Rotten lower leaves...............indicate *overwatering*

Wilted leaves and wet compost......indicate root rot by *overwatering*

Fallen buds and flowers............indicate *overwatering* or *too dry an atmosphere*

Green slime on pot.................indicates *overwatering or high humidity*

White deposit on pot..........indicates *overfeeding*

Too dark or lanky new growth.......indicates *overfeeding*

Grey mould on leaves and stems .....indicates rot through *too much humidity*

Browning leaf edges.................can be caused by *excess direct sunlight* or *a potash deficiency*

Question 2: What did I do wrong, Doctor?

Answer: You probably didn't do enough. Look for plant signs of too little water/underfeeding/draughts/not enough light. They are:

Browning leaf edges.................can also be because of *cold draughts*

Unusually small, dark new leaves...indicate *underwatering*

Wilted leaves and stems............indicate *underwatering* or *disease*

Shedding of older leaves...........indicate *underwatering*

Patches of brown or yellow leaves..indicate *underfeeding*

Stunted growth.....................indicate *underwatering* and *underfeeding*

Variegated leaves reverting to yellowish green...indicate *insufficient light*

Spindly growth.....................indicates *insufficient light*

Twisted leaves turning desperately towards light source...undoubtedly *insufficient light*

Elaborate diagnosis is not always necessary. In Arctic winters a plant in a cold room (especially if it's on a window sill) can simply freeze to death. The drier it is, the more cold it will tolerate, so in the winter keep the plant dry.

Bottled gardens

One of the healthier things a working girl can have in a bottle is a garden.

A garden in a bottle (the proper name is terrarium) is a miniature garden growing inside a very small greenhouse. The plants are protected from draughts, dust, sudden changes in temperature, excess moisture or dryness, tobacco smoke, and central heating. They will flourish almost indefinitely with the right sort of neglect.

First choose your bottle - an old sweet jar, glass storage jar, screw-topped honey jar, goldfish bowl or whatever. Huge jars with narrow necks look marvellous but are fiddling to

Tradescantia, Kalanchoe, African violets and a spider plant make a garden out of a kitchen jar.

plant, because you have to poke the plant in with a fork or back-scratcher. Goldfish bowls should be covered over at the top with a plate of glass or sheet of polythene kept in place with a rubber band.

Put a few little stones in the bottom of the bottle for drainage, then put in a layer of FISONS COMPOST. Add a little moss for theatrical effect, and bed the plants in with a spoon or fork. If the sides of the bottle get dirty, in the process, take a swab of clean cotton wool, dip in water and run it round the inside of the bottle with a pair of tongs or tweezers.

Don't stand your terrarium in bright sunlight.

Good plants for bottling are small ferns; Tradescantia, with elegant pale-green leaves; Kalanchoe, which has jagged dark-green jungly leaves and tiny orange flowers; African Violets.

You can, of course, buy your garden already bottled.

Bottle gardens have been around for well over a century. They work because the moisture taken in by the plants at the roots is given off from the leaves as vapour, but it isn't dissipated into the atmosphere - it condenses on the sides of the jar and runs down to moisten the soil and the roots again. You make your own rain. And so on. The whole process repeats itself as long as the top is kept on the bottle almost all the time.

The trick of preserving the garden is to leave it alone. The only care necessary is to take the top off the bottle occasionally for a treat on a Sunday afternoon *for a few hours only* to prevent condensation. Chop the plants back with nail scissors if they show signs of growing out of the bottle (some people call this pruning).

131

How to grow an avocado jungle

It gives quite a feeling of achievement to grow your own avocado tree. First eat your avocado. Then put the stone in a dish containing half an inch of water. Leave the dish in a cool, dark corner of your kitchen and every time you eat another avocado, put the stone in the dish, because only 1 seed in 5 'takes'.

When this happens, a white root grows out of the blunt, bulbous end of the stone; don't forget that it's the rounded part, that *looks* like a bottom, which is the part it should be sitting on.

You can then take the stone away and poise it over a jar or bottle of water, by jamming it in with matchsticks.

Keep the bottle full of water so that the bottom of the avocado is always wet. Put it in a sunny place, but not in front of the kitchen window where it's draughty. When the stem is 12 inches high and has several leaves, transplant it into a flower pot. This should be done when it's 4 months' old.

Don't keep the plant in very hot

sunshine. See that it has plenty of water in summer and don't overwater it in winter. Within a year you should have a plant about 2 foot high, and eventually it may reach the ceiling, although sadly it won't ever fruit, and you'll never get a decent shape from an avocado seed plant. They'll have a tall stem and look straggly, but they're FUN.

How to plant indoor bulbs

Daffodils, hyacinths, narcissus, tulips, crocus and snowdrops should be planted as early as possible in autumn, for winter and spring flowering. So-called "prepared" bulbs have already been heat-treated and must be planted immediately you buy them.

Put the bulbs in boxes; cover them with peat, sand or bark - not straight soil.

Place the bulb boxes in a place that's as dark and cold as possible - preferably outside and unprotected.

When the first sprouts appear, gradually bring in the bulbs - perhaps from the cold outdoors to cold greenhouse or cellar, then to a warmer indoor temperature, with light.

Transfer bulbs to pots, planting in potting compost (JOHN INNES NO.3). If you are using pots with drainage holes, put broken crockery at the bottom of the pot, as with other indoor plants.

If planting in undrained bowls, use bulb fibre. The bulbs can be planted close together, nearly touching, and the tips should just show above the surface.

Start watering when you want the bulbs to grow, which may take 6 weeks in a warm atmosphere.

Don't throw away bulbs in pots or bowls, after they have flowered; plant them out of doors.

Growing indoor plants from seed

You can grow indoor plants from seed in spring for at least six times less than you pay in the shops. And they make good presents. Try Busy Lizzie (pretty pink flowers): umbrella plant (elegant palm-like leaves): Flame Nettle (Coleus, with multi-coloured leaves). Order them from THOMPSON AND MORGAN or SUTTONS LTD. (see address book p. 112)

You'll need a plastic seed tray, a pane of glass large enough to cover it, a small bag of soil-less seed compost, a bag of JOHN INNES NO.1 potting compost, and eight each of 2-inch and 6-inch diameter pots.

The night before sowing, fill the tray with seed compost and firm. Immerse in sink, so water almost reaches rim. Leave until the compost begins to show darker, then drain.

Don't sow the seeds too thick or too deep: just press seeds into the surface, then cover the tray with glass and a sheet of paper. Put in the light (but not direct sunlight) and keep the tray warm.

Turn over the glass once daily and wipe off condensation. Seedlings should appear in 7 - 28 days.

As soon as you see the seedlings remove the glass and paper or you'll lose the seedlings. Then water the tray when necessary, by plunging in sink again.

When seedlings are ½ inch in height, transplant to small pots filled with potting compost. Water them in to settle them down in the pot.

When the plant's roots spread right through the compost, transplant them to larger pots. Feed with liquid fertilizer (PHOSTROGEN) when plants have been growing in the 6-inch pots for about 4 weeks.

Window boxes

"A garden is a wondrous thing to keep, even if it's just 6 inches deep".

Warning: A window box with absolutely nothing growing in it, standing on a window-sill can block out up to 15% of the light coming through an average window. By the time you've managed to *grow* something a quarter of the light may be shut out. So make up your mind whether you want light or flowers. If light, plant the box with sprawling waterfalls of greenery and flowers that spill over the edge of the sill instead of climbing up. The snag is that you won't see the flowers - the people on the opposite side of the road will, but it may encourage them to start their own.

Make sure your window box is at least 6 inches deep and 6 inches wide, and fits your window-sill as near as possible - securely fastened so that it won't fall on you, or passers-by. There are some excellent, light, fibre-glass window boxes that look like lead boxes used in the 18th Century, or you can buy a cheap, chain-store plastic, window box in nasty green and paint it some other colour.

If you haven't a window-sill to support your box it's possible to screw brackets into the wall under the window, but make sure they're safe.

Put broken pottery into the bottom of the box (if you haven't broken any lately, smash a few flower pots), and cover them with fibrous or dead leaves, then fill the box with JOHN INNES NO.2 compost. You're supposed to let the soil settle for 10 days or so before planting.

Remember that flowers will turn to face the sun, so choose those that are pretty from both sides. If you have a sunny window-sill plant:

snap-dragons (antirrhinum) in pink, yellow or crimson:

geraniums in red, white or pink:

small pink or blue hydrangeas:

lobelia (that blue stuff which looks like veiling on Edwardian hats):

petunias - small purple or white trumpets:

stocks, which smell romantic, are prettiest in lavender, pink or purple:

verbena, with its wonderful smell of soap:

wallflowers in yellow, *sang de boeuf* or velvety smart browns:

small spring bulbs such as blue muscari or crocus, in lavender, white or yellow (which birds prefer).

Window boxes that have currently lasted me eight years are planted with little laurel bushes, because I wanted a permanent, waxy dark green that gave no trouble: in between them, I plant whatever is seasonal.

For a waterfall of trailing plants down the front of the house, plant ivy-leaved geranium, honeysuckle, ivy, periwinkle and tradescantia.

Once a week remove dead flowers and yellowing leaves. Thoroughly water the window box, or even more frequently in hot weather. Use a watering can with a narrow spout, so you don't wash the soil away through the draining holes of the box. If the soil starts going green, get a little hydrated lime from a nursery and fork it in. Fork the soil surface over gently before feeding your plants with a liquid fertilizer, such as BABY BIO or LIQUINURE.

FLOWER POWER

I could no more pick a flower out of my garden than I could wrench an arm off one of my children, but I don't feel so personal about flowers I don't know. Whatever flowers you acquire, whether from your own patch of earth, or a friend's or from the florist, it's worth knowing how to arrange them to look their prettiest, and to last as long as possible.

The first rule of flower arranging is that there are no rules. Always remember that you're doing flowers for *you* and *your* home - not decorating an old fashioned hat at someone's wedding, or an office reception desk: ignore old fashioned rubbish about flowing line, crescent-shaped arrangements, dark colours at the base of the container, following the central line, and so on. Don't inhibit your enjoyment by worrying about what is preached in those complicated, traditional flower arranging books. Consider only the following practical points.

1. Visualize what you want, in your mind's eye. Arrange them fast and steadily and if they look fairly good, leave them. Don't try to rearrange, it hardly ever works. Start again with a different idea.

2. If you're buying flowers, buy sensibly - in bud but not so tightly that they're unlikely ever to open. Flowers in season are obviously cheaper than out-of-season ones, and healthier and better looking, as perhaps they won't have had such a long journey to reach you. Buy a mass of inexpensive flowers rather than a few costly blooms. A huge bunch of purple-to-crimson ane-

mones plunged into a white pudding basin will look more exuberant than half-a-dozen lacklustre naked carnations in a cut-glass vase. But then you say, what about a single spray of Madonna lilies or lilac in a bottle. Quite right; you see there are *no* rules.

3. Be brave. If you have a garden use *everything* from it; don't look down on weeds, seed-heads, berries or vegetables. You might, like David Hicks, have bunches of watercress or parsley in a shallow container, as a base for a centrepiece. You might use vegetable foliage, such as carrot tops, or red or silver grey cabbage leaves as a base for pinkish flowers or just one spray of asparagus in a bottle to hold it upright. If the bottle isn't pretty, hide it in a vase.

If you have no garden and rely on florist's flowers, don't try to do rural posies - try geometric, slightly artificial arrangements which rely on the flowers being all the same size, shape and colour. It's easiest to get good effects with flowers all the same colour, or in the same range of colours. The safest groups are reds/oranges/yellows: blues/violets/creams: greens and whites. If you match them to the predominating colour in the room you're bound to triumph.

4. Use dried grasses, gypsophila, bulrushes, fennel, hydrangea heads (lovely), dried thorns, dried leaves for a build-up of brown, beige, background colour. Use the seasonal accessories of the countryside - twigs, branches. Simple beech leaves always look lovely, so do sprays of berries, ferns or pussy willow used boldly by themselves.

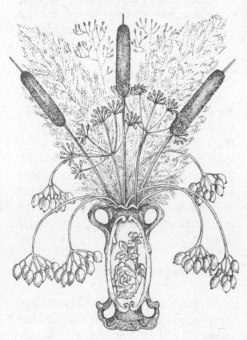

5. Ignore over-elaborate, cut-glass vases. They tend to look pretentious. Beware of wide, too shallow bowls, however charming.

6. Choose helpful vases. 'Containers' are what people call them since they started going in for old lavatory bowls, copper kettles, horse troughs and so on. A helpful container is one which is the right size, a good shape and solidly balanced.

Use everyday kitchen objects, a celery glass, soufflé dishes, glass jam jars, water jugs and carafes, earthenware kitchen jars, plain white china kitchen jugs, empty green glass bottles. Stems of trailing jasmine look particularly lovely falling from a Woolworths plain-stemmed wine glass and I sometimes float flowers in a saucer or glass finger bowl, using white chrysanthemums, water lilies, daisies. (It doesn't look as twee as it sounds).

137

Vases which open out like trumpets look very pretty but are difficult to make flowers behave obediently; great bulbous pots with narrow necks make whatever flowers you put in them look weedy and undersized; all jugs and decanters are fine; most bowls are charming, if they're deep enough and you have flowers to fill them: I'm afraid I have a weakness for classic silver rose bowls, with their own little gratings in the middle.

Keep your containers simple. If there's a line to the container follow it. Use very simple container shapes, because you can't fail to get a good little arrangement with them. Use cylindrical glass vases or tumblers and drinking glasses: (very good for a single flower with one leaf).

No arrangement is too small or insignificant to look pretty - a single rose in a tonic water bottle, two big daisies in an egg-cup, some snow-drops in a sherry glass.

7. Don't bother with crumpled chicken wire to hold your flowers in place; either do without and let the flowers fall naturally where they will, or buy those crumbly green bricks of foam "oasis" from a florist, then cut a chunk to fit.

Japanese pinholders are fine for doing Japanese arty-crafty arrangements - making two chrysanthemums and a dead twig look devastatingly preconceived - but you'll never see anything like that in my home.

8. When arranging the flowers make sure you have plenty of counter space, a chopping board, a sharp pair of secateurs, a hammer (or shoe heel) for thick stalks, scissors for soft stalks, a water jug - with a good long spout, for adding water to the container after you've arranged the flowers in it.

A quick way to cut flowers to the length that looks all right in the container. Put the container on the counter or table, hold the bunch of flowers against it, in front of the counter and raise or lower them while the proportion looks right. Then snip. Don't be afraid to cut down long stems drastically; (the shorter the stem the longer the flower will last) and try breaking up sprays into single flowers.

To preserve cut flowers in water

Daffodils, other bulb flowers and thin stems: Cut 1 inch off stem, cutting at an angle.

Hard-stemmed, such as chrysanthemums: Bash bottom 4 inches of stems, or they can't absorb water.

Very hard-stemmed, such as lilac or roses: Strip off any thorns from stem. Split or crush stem end with a hammer, rolling pin, heel of shoe, or whatever. Snip up the centre of stem for two inches. Plunge to neck in cold water. Roses are very time consuming (so never give them as a gift to your hostess unless she has a spare twenty minutes, rather than being about to serve a meal). On my fiftieth birthday my very first boyfriend sent me fifty 4-foot long roses and I had to wrestle with them in the bathroom, which needed entirely re-cleaning by the time I'd finished. If you leave leaves on the flower stems below the water-line, your glorious creation will stink unappealingly of stagnant weedy water. Strip the stems, because they're easier to manage that way.

Cut daffodils but crush rose stems to preserve in water.

Keep the water pure by throwing in a drop of bleach or a small teaspoon of salt, and an aspirin in the water really does work. Make the flowers last longer by adding a pinch of PHOSTROGEN (fertilizer powder used in the garden). Susan Pulbrook, who arranges the flowers at Buckingham Palace, says don't bother to change the water but *top it up* with fresh water, daily if you can. Don't stand flowers in a draught or near a radiator or your flowers will open very fast and your creation will start looking overblown before you've got used to seeing it.

To revive a wilting flower arrangement: Re-cut ends of stems and stand in 1 inch of boiling water for a few seconds, then give the flowers a long drink, up to the neck, in cold water for a few hours.

Don't throw the flowers away too soon, just because it's customary. Try watching the whole life-cycle, with blossom falling, petals fluttering down, leaves crumpling and the whole arrangement changing colour. I exasperate my mother (who is a trained, trad. florist) by saying "No, don't take those tulips away, I'm watching them die". Decay can be very pretty.

Finally, if you're buying flowers as a gift, why not be original? They can buy their own dreary gladioli, *you* can send or take one purple orchid in a filmstar cellophane box, or a bunch of evil black-and-green snakeshead irises wrapped in black tissue paper, or enough Michaelmas daisies to fill a soup tureen. If you want to play safe, send white flowers which look great in any setting.

Don't be original if you're taking flowers to someone in hospital because hospitals never have the right sort of vase.

Avoid roses because the patient will have no hammers in hospital, and often no shoes. Take a plant in a container or a small posy of garden flowers, nothing over-scented and nothing big, because there may not be room for it beside the bed.

Index

SOME USEFUL LENGTHS
(Imperial and metric measurements)

(1 centimetre = 10 millimetres = 39 inches)

(1 metre = 100 centimetres = 3.28 feet)

¼ inch = 6.35 millimetres	1 foot = 30 centimetres
½ in = 12.7 mm	1½ ft = 46 cm
¾ in = 19 mm	3 ft = 91 cm
1 in = 25.4 mm	
3 in = 76.2 mm	3½ ft = 1.07 metres
6 in = 152 mm	4 ft = 1.22 m
8 in = 203 mm	6 ft = 1.83 m
9 in = 229 mm	10 ft = 3.05 m